# CONTENTS

# LIKE A MIGHTY ARMY

### VICTOR MAXWELL

LIKE A MIGHTY ARMY
© Copyright 2005 Victor Maxwell

ISBN  0 900903 81 3

Printed and Published by

**biblical**
**BOO🗸S**

**jc** print ltd
BELFAST

Telephone 07860 205333
Fax 028 9079 0420

# 1

## LIKE A MIGHTY ARMY

It was with some pride and prestige that young Florisvaldo made it through all his rigorous training to finally qualify as a Military Police officer. Wearing the light blue uniform gave him a measure of self-esteem and importance. These early days gave no warning that Florisvaldo's self-esteem would turn to shame and the colourless apparel of the State penitentiary would replace his police uniform. This young man who came from the rural hinterland of Sao Paulo would become notorious and be convicted of some of the most grievous crimes in the recent history of Brazil.

During his time in the military police Florisvaldo was placed in a poor and violent district of Sao Paulo, Brazil's most populous city and the third largest city in the world. While there he was struck by the intensity of the violence he faced daily, "I started working as a police officer in a very calm town inland. When I was nineteen years old I was appointed to work in the city of Sao Paulo. I wasn't psychologically prepared to face such extreme violence every day.

It shocked and traumatised me so much I decided I would carry out justice myself."

From 1981 to 1983 Florisvaldo took the law into his own hands and started killing those he judged should die: criminals and suspected criminals. Newspapers, not knowing who the phantom executioner was, coined the nickname "Cabo Bruno" (Corporal Bruno) for him. Nobody really knows how many people died in these summary executions. Some reports say twenty, others say there were as many as thirty or fifty murders. At the height of the media furore a figure as high as one hundred was reported by some. Florisvaldo himself does not know how many were killed. Whenever a criminal was found dead in suspicious circumstances in the Sao Paulo area, the media quickly accorded the blame to Cabo Bruno. Some of these accusations were true, and some were not.

Cabo Bruno was first captured in 1983. Three times he was able to escape prison before being ultimately put behind bars in 1991. By that time there was loud public clamour in Brazil to have Bruno off the streets and in permanent custody. At court, even though the Brazilian justice system usually gives a maximum sentence of 30 years to the heinous criminals, Cabo Bruno was sentenced to a one hundred and twenty-year jail term. He was sent to the high security prison, Anexo de Casa Custodia, where the country's most feared criminals were detained in a regime that was notoriously horrible.

"I was kept in solitary and was totally desperate," said Florisvaldo of his time there. "Every day I heard the prisoners chanting aloud *"Cabo Bruno is going to die; Cabo Bruno is going to die; Cabo Bruno is going to die."* Lying alone in a small cell, in living conditions he could never have imagined, he began to consider taking his own life. He did not want to die at the hands of his enemies, and he knew that despite all the security, many of his fellow prisoners had plans to kill him soon and would delight in doing so. However, God had different plans for Florisvaldo.

In 1991 a Dutch lady visited Brazil, and as she watched the news on TV the story of Cabo Bruno caught her attention. She decided to send him a Bible with a letter telling him that Jesus loved him despite all the horrendous crimes he had committed. Florisvaldo did not come from a religious background. He had never cared about God in the past and had actively disliked professing Christians. Notwithstanding his past, Florisvaldo decided to read that Bible as the last hope for his life. He read the Bible through in a very short time. The story of how God forgave all the sins of Israel made a deep impression on him. The words of Isaiah 1:18 seemed to be an invitation to him: "Come now, and let us reason together, saith the Lord: though your sins be as scarlet, they shall be as white as snow; though they be red like crimson, they shall be as wool." Consequently, Florisvaldo cried out to God for mercy and forgiveness.

A short time after this another lady from Sao Paulo wrote to Florisvaldo about God's love and forgiveness. Besides writing, this lady also travelled up to meet Florisvaldo at the prison. During her visit she discovered that the penitent prisoner had already been transformed by the grace of God. The lady encouraged Florisvaldo to start telling his fellow prisoners the good news. He explained to her that the great difficulty of doing this was that for his own safety he was kept separate from the other prisoners. The lady assured him that she would pray for him.

Florisvaldo decided he would speak to his fellow prisoners by getting down on the floor and talking to them from under the cell door. Little by little he gained the confidence of the men who had previously planned to kill him. Because of his isolation he never did see the faces of those men, but by the time he left that prison thirty-six of the forty prisoners on that wing, took time out every night to hear Florisvaldo read and explain the Word of God.

In 2002 Florisvaldo was transferred to a special prison for former police officers where he remains today. In this penitentiary he has found many open doors to share his faith with former fellow officers. Now Florisvaldo leads a church behind bars. The church has its own music group and deacons. His friends at the prison don't call him Cabo Bruno any more. They now call him Pastor Florisvaldo. It all began with one copy of the Bible.

The Bible is undoubtedly a miracle book. There is no other volume quite like it. It has rightly been hailed as the Monarch of all books. The drive for global literacy and the proliferation of multiple publications in numerous languages has not dislodged the Bible from still being the world's best-selling book. More copies of the Bible are in circulation today than any other volume. The Bible which is one of the oldest pieces of printed classics, is unrivalled in the number of languages into which it has been translated, and these Holy Scriptures have affected and transformed more lives than any other piece of literature.

While my wife, Audrey, and I were working in the interior regions of the Amazon as missionaries, we were amazed at the power of the Word of God on an entire community. One memorable incident from before our time resulted in a whole town opening up for the establishing of an evangelical church. It is quite a number of years ago when a lone colporteur arrived by canoe in this remote town carrying a supply of Bibles, New Testaments and gospel booklets. Although his visit to the Boca do Acre was received with much suspicion and apprehension, he was able to distribute his literature and sell several Bibles and New Testaments. Some forest dwellers even hailed his canoe to the edge of river so they could purchase copies of the precious Word of God.

However, as soon as the anonymous colporteur pointed his canoe back down river, the town's resident Italian Roman Catholic priest, who had been greatly angered by the visit of the evangelist, announced to his flock that all the "Protestant literature" was of the devil and must be brought to the church. When the priest recovered as much of the literature as he could, he torched the Bibles and booklets in a public bonfire at the town square in front of the church.

Providentially, not all the Bibles were turned into ashes. Some scriptures found their way into simple homes scattered throughout the forest region. These ignited a different flame that would burn in the hearts of the readers for years to come.

Senhor Pedro and his family lived deep in the forest, several days' journey from Boca do Acre, the town visited by the Bible colporteur.

Like most of the people who lived in these isolated places, Pedro made his meagre living from extracting latex from the syringa trees and gathering Brazil nuts in January and February. To adequately provide for his family, he supplemented his scant income by hunting in the jungle and fishing in the lakes and rivers.

One day while hunting, he came upon a deserted and derelict hut deep into the forest. Having a keen eye for anything the former and unknown residents might have left behind, Pedro searched through the dust and debris of the abandoned shack. The only thing he found was an old Bible, one of those which had been sold by the itinerant servant of God. Not only was the old black book covered in dust, the busy termites had feasted on the torn cover and had burrowed their way through some of its pages. Pedro picked up the abandoned Bible, blew the dust off the cover and slowly began to read the words, "Biblia Sagrada".

Pedro was semi-literate but he knew that this was a holy book. He placed the Bible into his latex covered bag which held his hunting rations and continued his pursuit of wild boar or deer to provide food for his family.

When the hunt had finished, Pedro returned to his simple forest dwelling which consisted of little more than a bamboo floor and a palm-leaf roof. At the time of the evening novena Pedro gathered his wife and children around to read to them from the holy book he had found in the forest. Slowly and hesitantly he pronounced each syllable as Pedro began to read the gospel to his family for the first time. These stammering readings continued every evening at the same hour. After reading, Pedro prayed simple but sincere prayers for his family. This family, like many others in the region, had never met a Christian nor seen a missionary, but the Bible made a profound impact on their lives. One evening Pedro told his wife, "I don't know what we have to do, but I believe Jesus Christ died to forgive and save us. Let us ask God for His forgiveness."

Pedro experienced a new peace in his heart. He also developed an increased appetite for reading the scriptures, which he often did by the dim light of a little kerosene lamp. His daily readings from the Bible made him wonder who could explain more of this holy book to him. He and his wife wanted their children to know the truth and enjoy a better life than the hard times they had experienced as forest-dwellers. Because of these aspirations they moved to live on the outskirts of Boca do Acre. Pedro and his wife also began to pray that God would send someone who could explain more about God and His Word.

Pedro's prayers were an important hinge on a door which would swing open to allow James and Dorrie Gunning to go to Boca do Acre in 1952 and establish the first evangelical church in that town. During the next fifty years that church has grown, planted other congregations, sent out missionaries and pastors to other regions and still maintains a gospel witness. It all began with one copy of the scriptures in an abandoned house.

There is no doubt that the Word of God is powerful. Although the Psalmist David marvelled at the revelation of God in creation he was even more overwhelmed by the revelation of God in the scriptures. He said, "The law of the Lord is perfect, converting the soul: the testimony of the Lord is sure, making wise the simple. The statutes of the Lord are right, rejoicing the heart: the commandment of the Lord is pure, enlightening the eyes. The fear of the Lord is clean, enduring for ever: the judgments of the Lord are true and righteous altogether. More to be desired are they than gold, yea, than much fine gold: sweeter also than honey and the honeycomb" (Psalm 19:7-10).

Even though the Bible may be considered to be a miracle book and the Monarch of all books, yet this sacred volume is not without its enemies. Throughout the centuries antagonists of the Bible, some of whom were leaders of professed Christendom, have tried to ban the Bible from the hands of the common people or burn it out of existence. Others have used their vain ploy of higher criticism to try to destroy this written, inspired and foundational work of the Christian faith. Even today, the inspirational authority of the Bible and the accuracy of the divine text are under insidious attacks from those who attempt to detract from the Bible's supremacy or try to dilute its stamp of divinity.

For all of these assaults on the Holy Bible there is an abiding freshness on the sacred page. It is truly the revelation of God given by inspiration of God and preserved in the providence of God for this and coming generations.

Psalm 68 is a song of victory. Its lyrics major on the victorious Lord who suspends nature, subdues nations and supplies the need of His people. Verse 11 of this Psalm provides a very appropriate truth that has meaning far beyond the context of the chapter: "The Lord gave the word: great was the company of those that published it."

This statement affirms the source and great authority of the scriptures – "The Lord gave the word." In Genesis 1 we read how God spoke creation into existence: "And God said, Let there be light: and there was light…And God said, Let there be a firmament in the midst of the waters, and let it divide the waters from the waters…And God said, Let the waters under the heaven be gathered together unto one place, and let the dry land appear: and it was so."

God who spoke creation into being is also the God of revelation. The inspiration and composition of the Bible belong to God. Paul wrote, "All scripture is given by inspiration of God, and is profitable for doctrine, for reproof, for correction, for instruction in righteousness" (2 Timothy 3:16). Peter affirmed, "For the prophecy came not in old time by the will of man: but holy men of God spake as they were moved by the Holy Ghost" (2 Peter 1:21).

However, this verse from the Psalms not only indicates the source of the great authority of the scriptures, it also conveys something of the secret of the great army of God's servants who publish and proclaim that same Word – "great was the company of those that published it." The word translated "company" indicates that those who publish this Word are likened to an army. God's strategy is to mobilise His servants as a great army to spread the Word.

An army -- what an appropriate picture for those who publish the Word of God. Like the columns of a mighty military force stepping into centuries of spiritual conflict we can imagine the valiant lines of prophets, apostles, martyrs, missionaries, pastors and preachers who have heralded the great message of the Bible all around our world. Like battalions of committed infantry armed with pens and ink, which are superior and mightier than any two-edged sword, come the printers and publishers of the Word of God. They follow in the ranks of the great scribes who first penned the scriptures on papyrus scrolls, the copiers who accurately and painstakingly reproduced further editions of these early manuscripts to preserve the Word of God for succeeding generations. We salute the courageous translator, John Wycliffe, who was not only the Morning Star of the Reformation, but also the forerunner of an innumerable platoon of soldier-scholars who devoted shrouded years to translating the scriptures for the people. These translators needed the skills of William Caxton and the early printers to make the scriptures accessible and available to the general populace at reasonable cost. We do not lose sight of Mary Jones and her Bible who motivated publishers and inspired the Bible Societies to set up agencies for the distribution and circulation of the scriptures all over the world.

Also making their vital contribution to this great cause is the vast number of anonymous friends who remain in the background sustaining all this operation with their fervent prayers and faithful financial support. Their role is reflected in the story of Moses on the mountain sustaining Joshua by his intercessions: "So Joshua …fought with Amalek: and Moses, Aaron, and Hur went up to the top of the hill. And it came to pass, when Moses held up his hand, that Israel prevailed: and when he let down his hand, Amalek prevailed. But Moses' hands were heavy; and they took a stone, and put it under him, and he sat thereon; and Aaron and Hur stayed up his hands, the one on the one side, and the other on the other side; and his hands were steady until the going down of the sun" (Exodus 17:10-12).

This great company of committed and loyal soldiers, unified in the cause of Christ's Kingdom, has been God's strategy for publishing the Word of God throughout the generations.

Every Home Crusade follows in the succession of this great company. With the same conviction of heart, commitment to mission and confidence in God's promises that characterised its founder, Mr. Ernest Allen, the team at the Every Home Crusade factory in Belfast operates as a disciplined company which is wholly dedicated to publishing the Word. For that reason a primary emphasis is given to publishing the scriptures rather than books about the Bible. Others do this work adequately.

Every month over seventy tonnes of paper are transformed into colourful and attractive booklets and tracts. Over and above producing millions of copies of *The Gospel of John*, other booklets are also very popular. The *Way of Salvation* gives an overview of the Bible from a selection of some of its principal chapters. *The Light of the World* booklet plainly sets out God's love and remedy for needy sinners. Children's tracts have been very effective throughout Europe. Workers in multiple countries have welcomed the reproduction of the New Tribes abridged lessons, *Creation to Christ*, on illustrated flashcards.

These are only a few of the productions, which have been translated into more than ninety languages and sent to more than one hundred and twenty countries. Sending the literature out is looked upon as the sowing. Letters and reports that flow into the office testify of the great harvest being reaped in numerous countries. Lives have been transformed, families have been united, communities have been touched and new areas have been evangelised.

The Every Home Crusade team comprises twenty-eight workers at their factory in east Belfast. In addition to their work on the factory floor, the team meets regularly to pray through the pressing needs of each day and for the consignments of literature that are dispatched from the premises. Every Home Crusade is a faith mission trusting God to meet its needs. All overseas literature is sent without any charge for printing, transport or import duty to the respective countries. The yearly budget is in excess of £1,000,000 which means that the Crusade needs to receive on average £3,000.00 every day throughout the year. The team is grateful to all the supporters who reflect God's faithfulness in blessing this work.

The factory workers are greatly helped and encouraged by various volunteers who compile, pack into envelopes and help dispatch items that automated production cannot handle. Office staff attend to the administration of the factory and to the large volume of correspondence from all over the world. Besides letters from those who faithfully send in their support for the work, requests come in every day from missionaries, pastors, church leaders, evangelists and Christian workers for literature in numerous languages. To attend to these requests the workshop is a busy place. Various printing presses are rolling off colourful booklets and tracts; other machines cut, fold and bind the booklets and these are stacked into boxes at the end of the production line. The boxes are stored in an adjoining unit, 18-tonne of literature is then packed into 20ft containers and shipped all over the world.

However, the Every Home Crusade workers do not consider themselves to be an isolated unit. They are only part of this vast company of committed servants of our Saviour King. While the team publishes the Word at the factory, other divisions of the King's great army are engaged in spreading the scriptures across great frontiers.

This book highlights and brings together the ministry of twelve servants of God who share the same vision and passion of Every Home Crusade. They and many other unmentioned Christian workers engage in the same ministry with the same objective: to reach every home with the gospel of Jesus Christ.

The Lord gave the Word. Every Home Crusade exists so that people might receive it.

*Front Row* - Jill Campbell, Marty McAllister, Carol Adams, Samuel Adams, Clive Allen, Kathleen Allen, Heather Mercer, Myrtle Cooke.
*Second Row* - Junior Hilland, David Maitland, Arthur Darragh, Kenneth McCulla, Jackie Walker, Ernie McKeown, Billy Campbell, Robin McCulla.
*Back Rows* - Gary Bolton, Leslie Buchanan, Paul Roberts, Douglas Condell, Paul McGuigan, Stephen Walker, David Senior, David Megarry,
Timothy Millen, Stephen Roberts, Simon Wade, Stephen Collins, Gary Boal. *(Every Home Crusade Staff)*

# BOARD OF DIRECTORS

# 2

# FROM WEST FERMANAGH TO WEST AFRICA
## *with*
### *William and Rosalind Brown*

"It's a pain that won't go away," said an elderly immigrant who came to Ivory Coast from neighbouring Burkina Faso. "Our hearts won't heal easily."

"Our own neighbours were shouting, 'Kill them like chickens,'" cried another woman.

These poor immigrants had virtually leaped from the frying pan into the fire. In an attempt to flee from oppression they had walked into another African uprising. Ivory Coast was being convulsed into political instability with a rebellion in the northern part of the country that resulted in the all-too-familiar pattern of slaughter and mass murder. The country was on the brink of civil war.

A taxi driver wiped tears from his eyes as he described how paramilitaries broke down the front door of his house and trailed away his seven brothers. Only one returned. He later found his brothers' bodies dumped in a field on the outskirts of town with about fifty-five other twisted corpses piled on top of one another. The surviving brother said they had been taken to an open compound, told to lie on the ground and shot. Mercifully he was able to escape.

An uprising had pushed Ivory Coast's military ruler from power and some people were celebrating in the streets. No sooner had the cries of jubilation begun when ethnic and religious tensions exploded into violence in this West African nation.

For years Ivory Coast was spared the violence that convulsed its neighbours, steadied by a booming economy and a revered leader who managed to co-opt most of his opponents. However, times had changed. Political unrest had come to Ivory Coast and civil war seemed imminent and inevitable.

Just at that critical time William and Rosalind Brown wrote to their prayer partners:

It is with a heavy heart that we write to update you regarding the situation in Ivory Coast. On 19th September 2002 an attempted coup was carried out by a mutinous element within the military. Sadly since then hundreds have been killed and the entire north (largely Muslim area) of the country is being held by the Rebel Soldiers who are determined to overthrow the government and demand new presidential elections.

Last week West African leaders attempted to negotiate a cease-fire but unfortunately they were unsuccessful and have now returned home. The future does not look promising as we read reports like 'Ivory Coast on verge of Civil War,' etc. As a family we are fine and rejoice in God's protection and provision during these recent weeks. I (William) was in N. Ireland with our son Daniel visiting my elderly parents when the fighting broke out. As a result of the current unrest I was unable to return to Ivory Coast. Rosalind, with our children, Matthew, Esther and Cherith, were therefore, obliged to pack up the essentials and make a hasty retreat to Abidjan where

they were able to get a flight to Dublin last Saturday. (5th October)
All missionaries have evacuated at least to Abidjan or left the country. The mission schools have also been forced to evacuate. We are still struggling to come to terms with the events of the last few weeks. Our home and friends are in Ivory Coast and our hearts go out to them. However, we rest in the knowledge that our God is sovereign and is in control! He is working out HIS purposes. What can we do? PRAY! PRAY! PRAY!

This volatile situation in West Africa is a long way and a complete contrast to the quiet rural settings of the country villages in West Ulster from where William and Rosalind originate. William was born near Irvinestown, surrounded by the lakes of County Fermanagh. It was there he had one of the greatest privileges anyone could enjoy, that of being born into a Christian home. Both of his parents loved the Lord and his earliest memories of home are sitting on his father's knee while he read Bible stories to him. His mother then prayed with him each night. The influence of that Godly up bringing left an indelible mark on William's life for which he is forever grateful.

The initial impact of his parents' prayers and Bible instruction was when he trusted Jesus Christ to be his Saviour as a child of four. The conversion of an infant is to be highly prized rather than despised. Jesus said "Suffer little children to come unto me, and forbid them not: for of such is the kingdom of God" (Luke 18 v 16).

Although converted at that tender age, William did not understand everything about salvation. It was some years later when he was reading Isaiah 49:16, "Behold, I have graven thee upon the palms of my hands," that he received the assurance that he really was a child of God. This word dispelled any tormenting doubts or hesitation to say that he really did belong to the Saviour.

William wasn't everything he should have been as a child and teenager, but during those formative years he was always conscious of the hand of God upon his life. Time and time again he experienced, and needed to experience, the Lord's tenderness and compassion and patience.

One night in 1979 Mr Ernie Allen from Every Home Crusade visited Manoo Independent Methodist Church. It was the first time to meet this man of God and he made a great impression on William.

Pointing to a supply of gospel literature, Mr Allen said to young William, "Take as many as you can use, brother!" This was music to William's ears. As a young teenager William had written to various organisations who supplied tracts but they customarily only sent a small quantity which was usually exhausted around the housing estates in Irvinestown in a short while. Off William went that night with a bundle of literature under his arm. Little did he know that twenty-five years later he would be looking for much larger quantities of literature from Every Home Crusade. After this initial contact with Ernie Allen, William's relationship with Every Home Crusade developed over the years.

In the rural areas of West Ulster many young people have to leave home to seek employment. However, when William was eighteen years old he joined the full-time Reserve of the Royal Ulster Constabulary (RUC). For the next four years William served as a police officer in Enniskillen, Kinawley, Belcoo and Kesh RUC stations, all in County Fermanagh. These years were at the height of Ulster's 'troubles' and Fermanagh's frontier stations often came under attack. It was an extremely dangerous region for all police officers and meant that William was very vulnerable to terrorist aggression.

On two occasions while he was on duty the Station in which he was serving came under mortar bomb attack. The first was at the Enniskillen RUC Training Depot in September 1985 and later at Belcoo RUC Station in April 1987. God spoke to William through those menacing incidents and he was conscious and confident that the Lord had protected him for a purpose.

As a young police officer he had everything a young man could wish for yet he lacked the peace and assurance that he was in the centre of the will of God. From his earliest years William had always been taught that God had a specific plan and a purpose for his life. He had also been repeatedly challenged at various meetings to surrender his life completely to God. Moreover, he was aware of the danger of 'settling down' and of missing God's plan by becoming content with lesser things. Over a period of time God brought William to the place of absolute surrender. To find and do the will of God not only became his greatest longing and desire, but also the first priority of his life.

When we surrender our will to God's will the Lord has a way of engineering our circumstances and ordering our every step. Following that crisis of surrendering to God and His will, the Lord brought a number of people across William's path who would make a profound influence on his life.

One was a Godly pastor who believed in the power of prayer. The pastor's life and ministry radiated his complete dependence on God.

William met another person who would have an even more lasting and deeper impression on his life. This was Rosalind Rooney, a beautiful girl from the lovely village of Florencecourt.

Rosalind was the youngest of four children born to Bertie and Betty Rooney. Her father was a farmer in Florencecourt and her mother a Primary School teacher.

Both parents were Christian believers and were very sincere and diligent in teaching their children in the things of God. Not only were the children sent to Sunday School and children's meetings, and attended many missions, but they were also taught God's Word in their home.

Although Bertie Rooney was a quiet man, yet he was a man of prayer and of deep spiritual convictions. At home he set a great example to his children and was held in great respect by them to the extent that they were loath to disobey or grieve him.

Rosalind's earliest memories are of her father gathering the children around a bedside each evening and unhurriedly reading God's Word to them. He encouraged the children to ask questions and did his best to explain the truths of Scripture in a way that a child could understand. He also encouraged the children to pray aloud independently as soon as they were able.

Bertie Rooney believed in the power of prayer, and when he had a concern about any of his children, it was not unusual for him to spend a half-day out in a field or shed, praying until he had a peace about the issue.

Because he was hard of hearing Bertie was not always aware when someone entered the room. When Rosalind was older she arrived home from school on many occasions to find that her father was praying aloud. Rosalind felt such an atmosphere of God in the room that she didn't know whether she dare make a sound, and yet she didn't want to eavesdrop on his private prayer time. Now, years later, Rosalind believes that God continues to answer her father's prayers even though he is at home with the Lord.

It was when Rosalind was seven years old that she became deeply conscious of her own sinful condition, and her need to trust in the Lord Jesus for salvation. She knew that her parents' faith was real, but that she needed to trust the Lord for herself. Rosalind knew that it was not simply the wrong things that she had done that separated her from God, but that she was by nature outside of God's family and needed to be saved.

On 4th March 1973 Rosalind attended a meeting in Enniskillen Independent Methodist Church with her parents. She listened intently and at the close of the meeting Rosalind responded to the gospel and indicated her desire to be saved. She still remembers how her great-uncle, Willie Moore, an Irish Evangelistic Band Evangelist, explained to her that a sinner was saved by faith in Jesus Christ, not by feelings and that she should never rely on how she felt, but simply trust Christ.

Following that meeting, while praying at home with her family, Rosalind repeatedly asked the Lord Jesus to come into her heart each time she prayed. Her dad seized the opportunity and opened Rosalind's Bible at Revelation 3:20, "Behold, I stand at the door, and knock: if any man hear my voice, and open the door, I will come in to him, and will sup with him, and he with me." He asked her if it was true that Jesus Christ had knocked at her heart's door and that she had let Him in. Establishing that this was indeed true, he followed by explaining that if Jesus was already living in her heart, she had no need to ask Him to come in again and again. That simple conversation marked the assurance that Rosalind needed that she really was a child of God.

Not long after her conversion, Rosalind had to write a story in school about what she wanted to do when she grew up. Rosalind had no problem with that one. Without hesitation she wrote that she was planning to be a missionary. Young Rosalind lost no time in becoming a missionary and tried to start there and then with her school friends. One day she came home and told her father that she had 'saved' one of her friends. Again, without making his daughter feel small, he explained that it was only God who could do the saving, but she could do the telling!

When Rosalind went up to the Collegiate school in Enniskillen she was greatly encouraged to meet several Christian friends of her own age. Having Christian companions made it much easier for each of them to stand against all the temptations that came their way for they were able stand together. They also had some fine Christian teachers who were a real encouragement.

The annual Church camps were one of the highlights of Rosalind's teenage years. She was challenged and blessed through good Bible teaching and was also introduced to several missionaries who had just come from their fields of service.

Enniskillen Independent Methodist Church to which the Rooney family belonged, was, and still is, a very missionary minded church. Rosalind looked forward to special missionary weekends with a mixture of anticipation and dread. She didn't want to miss a meeting and yet she was becoming increasingly aware that God was speaking to her personally about her willingness for overseas service.

She comforted herself with the thought that she needed to complete her education before having to really face up to the issue. Furthermore, since she planned to go on for further education that put the issue of possible missionary service on hold.

It was when Rosalind was contemplating leaving school, and thinking what she might do next, that God really brought the whole

matter of missionary work before her again. She had no doubt that
God had clearly led her to Stranmillis College to do a teaching degree.
Other doors that she had considered were closed. While she was
conscious of God's guiding hand on her life and circumstances, she
wondered in the back of her mind what would come next.

Far removed from the protective influence of her home for the
first time meant that Rosalind had freedom to spend her time as she
chose. Sadly, for a period of time her relationship with the Lord took
a back seat. Some of her fellow students professed to be Christians but
seemed to be able to live as they pleased, doing things that Rosalind
had never imagined could be consistent with being a Christian.
Rosalind was thrown into confusion and frustration. She seriously
questioned all that she had grown up with and wondered why on earth
she had spent so much time 'being different' if it was not really
necessary. These questions brought many doubts and made her feel
miserable.

While she wrestled with these doubts and questions Rosalind read
again from 2 Corinthians 5:17, "Therefore if any man be in Christ, he
is a new creature: old things are passed away; behold, all things are
become new." As she read and meditated on these words the mist
began to clear and her struggles ceased. She reasoned that if 'new'
really meant 'new' and 'all' really meant 'all', then there was no issue
to consider. As a Christian she was a new creature and old things had
passed away.

While still a student and emerging from these doubts, Rosalind
was greatly encouraged by reading the autobiography of Isobel Kuhn,
OMF missionary to China and Thailand. This veteran missionary also
went through a similar struggle as a young Christian. Indeed, Isobel
Kuhn became one of Rosalind's favourite authors and she has read and
reread all her books many times since then.

Rosalind's twenty-first birthday party, arranged by some of her
student friends, was a major milestone in her life. Not only had she
come of age but that party was to mark her first date with a young man
from Fermanagh, William Brown. However, Rosalind's plans were
thwarted.

William was in the security forces in County Fermanagh and at the last minute a security alert meant that his leave was cancelled. Instead of looking into Rosalind's eyes on this special prearranged date, William spent that evening on a covert operation lying in a ditch near to the border looking out for terrorist suspects.

There was no way William was going to let a RUC security operation spoil his intentions to win the heart of this lovely young girl. Not to be put off, he said he would go to Belfast on the following evening to meet his date. However, there was a problem. Rosalind was committed to attending a prayer meeting in Lisburn with some other young people on that night. Not wanting to miss her opportunity of going out on a date with Constable Brown, she wasn't sure what to do about the prayer meeting. She tentatively explained the situation to him. There was some sort of mutual determination that they should be with each other that evening but William would not hear of Rosalind missing the prayer meeting on his account. She was greatly relieved when William insisted that he would go to the prayer meeting with her.

It was very appropriate that the young couple's first date was to a prayer meeting for it set the tone for their relationship. Right at the beginning of their friendship they discovered that they shared a mutual keen interest in overseas missionary work. Subsequently, they spent many hours discussing various missions and the different fields of service they might be suited to and how God was guiding them. Together they took Matthew 6:33 as their motto, "Seek ye first the Kingdom of God and all these things shall be added onto you." In the succeeding years William and Rosalind have proved God's faithful promise time and time again.

This promise was put to the test in their lives in 1988 when God opened the way for William to go to Bible College. Since he had been protected and preserved through several terrorist incidents God had been speaking to him about serving Him 'full-time.' This call was confirmed at a farewell service for his pastor when Rev. Tom Cross brought a challenging message on "God's work and God's workers." William knew that night that God had called and he must obey.

When he announced his intentions to fellow officers in the RUC his comments were met with incredulous looks and unbelief. One lady asked him, "But how are you going to live?" Matthew 6:33 answered that question. If we look after God's business He will look after our business. After sixteen years in Christian work William gladly admits that he has lacked nothing for God is always faithful to His promises.

When William left for Bible College it meant that he had to leave County Fermanagh just as Rosalind got her first teaching post back in the Fermanagh village of Lisbellaw. It was a small price to pay in stepping out to serve the Lord.

••••

Besides his studies at Bible College William was exposed to various missionaries and mission representatives who visited the College. During one Missionary Weekend in Coleraine he heard Ed Norwood, a former UFM Worldwide missionary to Brazil and Irish representative of the Mission, speak from Revelation 14:4, "These are they which follow the Lamb whithersoever He goeth. These were redeemed from among men, being the firstfruits unto God and to the Lamb." Ed introduced his congregation to the work of UFM in Ivory Coast and challenged all present to "follow the Lamb whithersoever He goeth." It was a stirring message and left a mark on William's life.

Meanwhile, Rosalind was thoroughly enjoying teaching in Lisbellaw and having the opportunity to be back in Fermanagh at her home church, Enniskillen Independent Methodist, where she helped in Sunday School teaching. These months living at home with her parents would become a very precious memory for Rosalind, as a year and a half after their marriage, her father, Bertie Rooney, was killed in a farm accident.

After William finished Bible College the happy couple were married and moved to East Belfast. For the next four years William served as the minister at Bloomfield Independent Methodist Church. Rosalind secured a teaching post at Cairnshill Primary School in Newtownbreda and the newly weds settled in to a whole new lifestyle.

Although there were times when they really missed the green fields of Country Fermanagh this was compensated for by making many precious and lasting friendships amongst God's people in East Belfast.

When they moved to Belfast William received a letter from Ernie Allen offering to print a leaflet free of charge in order to introduce the Bloomfield Independent Methodist Church to the local neighbourhood. This kind and thoughtful gesture touched William and made the Fermanagh man feel that at least he had some friends in the 'big smoke!'

Not long after settling into their new accommodation in the city William introduced Rosalind to the Every Home Crusade factory in Redcar Street, also in East Belfast. She was amazed at how such a small place could turn out so much gospel literature to be sent all over the world. Mr. Ernie Allen had been a frequent visitor at Rosalind's home church in Enniskillen where he had a special relationship with Mr George Hamilton who was a former Sunday School superintendent at the church. After seeing the EHC factory of which she had heard so much and prayed for so often, Rosalind had the same reaction as the Queen of Sheba meeting Solomon, "I believed not the words, until I came, and mine eyes had seen it: and, behold, the half was not told me" (1 Kings 10:7).

During their four years in East Belfast, the awareness that one day they would serve God overseas never left them. Ed Norwood kept in regular contact with them and often would say, "I just want you to know I am praying for you every day."

Although the church work in East Belfast was uppermost in their minds, yet they became particularly interested in the Ivory Coast through their contacts with UFM and through reading Patrick Johnson's 'Operation World'. Sometimes it seemed to be at the forefront of their minds and they talked of little else. At other times the interest in Ivory Coast faded because life had become so busy. This was especially the case after the arrival of their first son, Matthew. Thoughts about Ivory Coast and UFM seemed to recede into the background and they wondered if they had been imagining that God had been tugging upon their hearts.

However, the burden for mission fields never left them. They were always challenged by the fact that so many people still needed to hear the gospel for the first time. That challenge constrained them to continue to be surrendered to God's will. For William and Rosalind the big question was "When" and "Where"? As they prayed they were assured that step-by-step the Lord would open up the way for them.

In the process of time God spoke through circumstances. During one particular week when they were very definitely asking the Lord to confirm if He would have them apply for missionary service in Ivory Coast, William was startled when 'Ivory Coast' cropped up in two separate conversations during two pastoral visits that week. God also spoke to them through His word in Romans 15:20 "Yea, so have I strived to preach the gospel, **not where Christ was named**, lest I should build upon another man's foundation:"

During the time William and Rosalind were praying about the whole matter of God's call to West Africa they attended another UFM weekend where a visiting missionary shared about his ministry in Vavoua International School in Ivory Coast. The Lord stirred their hearts again and they were eager to do His will.

Following the missionary weekend Rosalind was doing a routine break duty in Cairnshill Primary School. Because it was raining the children were inside so Rosalind was supervising a few classrooms in one part of the school. As she wandered from room to room thoughts about Ivory Coast and God's call dominated her mind and she was inwardly praying that God would make His will so clear that they would be left in no doubt. Just then she was drawn to a wall display that she had never seen before in one of the classrooms. A closer look made her stop in her tracks. The display concerned an exchange of letters between the class and a former pupil in the school. The child was now a pupil in none other than Vavoua International School in the Ivory Coast and she was looking forward to coming home on furlough and rejoining the class for a time. Rosalind felt sure this was no coincidence but that God was indeed speaking personally to her.

While these musings were going on in their hearts God blessed William and Rosalind with the birth of their second child. Esther, a sister for Matthew joined the family. However, the birth of Esther made the Browns realise that the longer they stayed at home in Northern Ireland the more difficult it would be to step out for God.

Finally, convinced that God was calling them to Ivory Coast, they applied to UFM Worldwide in the autumn of 1993. Although they had a peace from God that they were stepping out in God's will yet they feared there was a huge mountain blocking their way. Since Ivory Coast is a French speaking country they would be required to attend language school in Paris for eighteen months. French was William's worst subject in school and he wondered how he could ever find the wherewithal to master this foreign tongue. He need not have feared for he discovered that when God calls a person to a task He equips that person with the necessary gifts and abilities. William maintains that had anyone told him then that one day he would be preaching and teaching in French, he would not have believed it, neither would his French school teacher.

Someone has said, "God does not call the qualified but He qualifies the called." William and Rosalind proved God's faithfulness and discovered that their impossibilities can become His opportunities.

Following application, interviews and candidates' time at UFM headquarters, they were accepted to serve the Lord in West Africa with the mission.

In order to free him to do deputation meetings, William left the Pastorate in 1994 and joined the staff of Every Home Crusade for several months where he worked in the packing department. He counted it a privilege to be involved in helping to send God's Word out all over the world! While there he enjoyed the fellowship with the factory team and established lasting friendships that would benefit his life and ministry for years to come. Furthermore, he got another education from the team when he entered into the daily discussions when anything from local politics to Calvinism versus Arminianism were on the agenda.

In 1995 they left for Language School in Massy, a suburb of Paris. The first term at language school was not easy for William and Rosalind. One of the rules of the school was that after a few weeks the student was only permitted to speak in French in the school! Coffee was served in bowls and William struggled to say, "Bonjour," or "Ca va?" while trying to concentrate on balancing his coffee at the same time, he then diplomatically moved on before the person had an opportunity to engage him in conversation! If the couple needed to speak to each other they had to find a private corner somewhere to communicate in English.

During their time in Paris, Rosalind also became involved in helping a Child Evangelism Fellowship club in the church they attended. Even though she felt she was unable to play an active part because of her limited French Rosalind really appreciated the experience of listening and watching the gospel being presented clearly to children in French.

In November 1996 Rosalind had a more profound lesson in French when she was admitted to a little clinic in Paris for the birth of their son, Daniel. The five days' enforced stay in the clinic gave Rosalind some of the best language experience she could have wished for.

••••

With language school in Paris behind them, it was with a sense of joy and anticipation that William and Rosalind and family started their first term in Ivory Coast in 1997. Initially they were based in Bouaké working alongside veteran missionaries to gain experience.

By trial and error many valuable lessons were learned during those early days and opportunities abounded to put their language skills into practice. One day William went to the door to greet their house girl, Salomé, who had been off ill for a few days. William thought he had asked, "You feel better?" She smiled but didn't reply. Later he discovered he had mixed up his verbs and had actually asked, "You smell better?"

Rosalind had been looking forward to working with and learning from an experienced children's worker with UFM, Miss Janis Tite. Janis had spent twenty fruitful years in Ivory Coast, but sadly, after only six weeks together, Janis had to return home because of a recurrence of cancer. This servant of God went to be with the Lord shortly afterwards. Before leaving Ivory Coast, Janis had entrusted to Rosalind the materials she had gathered up over her years of service. Rosalind felt that the Lord was passing the baton on to her, even though she was conscious of being very inadequate for the task.

UFM Worldwide works in partnership with an evangelical national Church in Ivory Coast. During their orientation period William had the privilege of working alongside a godly Ivorian pastor, Kahouotjiqué Koné and his wife, Anne-Marie. Koné came from the Northern Tagbana tribe and was burdened to reach his own tribe with the gospel. Each week William accompanied Koné to engage in the church work. They travelled extensively in an old Renault 12, which had served numerous missionaries before them.

William related how he was greatly encouraged by working alongside Pastor Koné:

> One Friday morning we were trying to find a village that had no evangelical witness. After driving up and down numerous dirt roads we got lost and decided to ask for directions from some men with machetes coming from working in their fields. They all came from the village that we were looking for and immediately offered to accompany us. Before we had time to respond they began to get into the car from all directions, including the boot.
>
> Pastor Koné explained that the car belonged to "the white man" and we only had room for another three passengers. About twelve of them had tried to crowd into the car. After the pastor spoke to them several climbed out of the car and, somewhat against their will, remained behind.
>
> Pastor Koné has a unique gift of seizing every opportunity to speak about the Lord and this was one of them as we travelled along! When we arrived at the village he asked if they were willing to trust in Jesus as their Saviour. They said they were

and then he turned to me and said; "Now William, you pray
with them!"

I wasn't convinced that they understood the gospel but I
prayed asking the Lord to reveal Himself to them.  One of
those men, Albert, that day truly trusted Jesus to save Him
and later testified to being delivered from fear of evil spirits.
How glad we were that we lost our way that day and that
Albert found the living way.

In December 1998 William and Rosalind moved to the west of
Ivory Coast and were based in Guiglo, where they worked amongst the
Guéré people. These people are largely animistic in their religious
beliefs and live in fear of sorcery.

Shortly after their arrival in the town William and Rosalind
became friendly with a Liberian couple, Murphy and Sarah. They had
fled from Liberia in the '90s because of the war there.  Sarah gave
birth to twins but one of them fell ill and in trying to help with medical
treatment the Browns got to know them well.

Sadly the baby died but God had a wonderful way of bringing
good out of what appeared to be a tragedy.  The distraught couple went
to visit William and Rosalind soon after the death of their baby and
said they would like to attend the church the Brown family worked at.
Because they were English speakers and the church services were
conducted in French, William suggested holding a weekly Bible Study
with them.  They were very enthusiastic about this and soon William
and Rosalind began teaching them chronologically through the Bible.

God began to work in their lives and their hunger and desire for
God's Word became very evident. It was a memorable day for William
and Rosalind in June 1999 when the seeking couple trusted the Lord
as Saviour. Because of the war in Ivory Coast they later fled to Ghana
but are going on with the Lord.  The last William and Rosalind heard
of them was that they are praying about going into full-time Christian
work among boys and girls.

Rosalind was presented with great opportunities to conduct many
children's clubs.   She also began some basic Child Evangelism

training for Ivorian Christian workers. In all her work Rosalind could never get used to the sight of so many children eager to hear God's Word but who were being overlooked by the Christian Church. Ivorians love their children, but as in the same way that the children are fed what is left over after the adults are served at the table, the same attitude is adopted when it comes to spiritual matters. Rosalind tried to provide a lending library of suitable materials to help the Sunday School teachers, but she never seemed to have enough material to meet the need.

In March 2000 the Browns were blessed with the arrival of their fourth child, another daughter. Cherith was born in a mission hospital in the north of Ivory Coast. Thankfully she arrived safe and sound despite her mother having had severe malaria during the pregnancy. The malaria treatment had involved a quinine drip, which is not recommended in pregnancy and William and Rosalind were warned of the risks to the unborn baby. It was a dilemma for the missionary couple but they had no choice. God kept His hand on Rosalind and Cherith showed no ill effects at all.

During their Home Assignment in 2000 William and Rosalind learned that Every Home Crusade had been given the copyright from New Tribes Mission to print the Chronological Bible lessons for Sunday Schools. The lessons were illustrated on coloured flashcards with the text of each lesson printed on the reverse side. Rosalind had already obtained an original set of these from New Tribes Mission and had been using them. Through her experience in West Africa she became fully convinced of the need to teach the Bible chronologically and it was a real answer to prayer to see these lessons come off the printing press in EHC.

When they returned to Ivory Coast they obtained some samples of these lessons in English, and were able to assure the children's workers in Ivory Coast that these lessons would soon be available in French also, and at no cost.

••••

After fourteen months into their second term of service William and Rosalind experienced one of the highlights of their time in Ivory Coast, but this was quickly followed by a low that they never imagined they would reach. The highlight was a camp for village Sunday School teachers which was held in the town of Guiglo. Twenty-six men and women, recommended by the elders of their churches, came together for a four-day training course in presenting the gospel to children. A full-time CEF worker and another friend from Northern Ireland had gone out to Africa to help teach this course. It was a time of rich blessing and the answer to many prayers. The fellowship was rich and the instruction excellent.

Fully equipped with what they had learned, the teachers went back to their villages after the camp with borrowed materials to help teach the children. After the camp finished William and their young son Daniel planned a two-week visit to see William's ageing parents and have Daniel's eyes tested. They travelled on the same flight to the United Kingdom as the two friends who had come from Northern Ireland to teach the course.

Little did William know then that his planned visit to Northern Ireland for two weeks would turn out to be an extended Home Assignment of almost two years and that Rosalind and their other three children would join him and Daniel a short time later.

During William and Daniel's visit to County Fermanagh some dramatic reports broke which were to change their plans. "Some fighting has broken out again and there has been an attempted coup." This was the news William heard from Rosalind over the phone on 19th September 2002.

Two days after William's departure from Ivory Coast news broke in Ivory Coast of an attempted coup d'etat. This was not the first such news since the Browns arrived in the country and Rosalind did not take it too seriously initially. However, as news came in that town after town had fallen to the rebels and the death toll was rising Rosalind began to wonder if it might be wise to think of going to the capital, Abidjan.

A female colleague in UFM had arrived to spend a few weeks with Rosalind and the children while William and Daniel were gone, before making her own way back to the UK on furlough. While she was there they tuned in to the BBC World Service and wondered what to do.

They comforted themselves with the thought that there were French families at a nearby sawmill who would certainly contact them if they felt it necessary to leave. When Rosalind and her friend saw a light aeroplane fly over one morning they joked that perhaps it had come to get them. It was then that they decided to contact the French families to see what their plans were. The two ladies were shocked to discover that the aeroplane they had seen overhead had been sent in by their timber company to evacuate the French women and children.

A curfew was declared in the town and all government offices were closed. Petrol was no longer available for sale and it became obvious to Rosalind that if she did not leave with her colleague, she could be stranded in the town. The two ladies read through the mission evacuation procedures and decided that they should follow them even though they both felt that the situation would not call for a complete evacuation, possibly only a short stay in the capital.

They got ready to leave early one morning with just enough petrol in the vehicle to make it to the capital, seven hours' drive away. They also decided to attach an Ivorian flag to the aerial as recommended on the national news and put their baggage in the boot of the car. When they tried to close the boot the lock seized and no amount of working at it would allow it to function again. Ever resourceful, a local friend got a strip of rubber cut from a tyre tube and tied the boot closed very firmly and the ladies with three children set off for Abidjan.

They were sure that many people at home were praying for them and that was the obvious reason why they had a very smooth journey through the multitude of checkpoints on the way to Abidjan. The ladies had taken with them a plentiful supply of EHC literature, gospels of John and tracts in French. At checkpoint after checkpoint they were able to distribute this literature and many soldiers asked them to pray for them and for the country. They discovered an openness that was greater than anything they had ever sensed before and found the people were very anxious about the future.

They passed many checkpoints where other people were made to get out of the car and unload the contents of the car's boot. On the only one occasion when the ladies were asked to open the boot of their car, they answered, "No problem. Just go ahead and open it."

When the soldier saw the complicated knots of rubber that held the boot closed he changed his mind and told them to drive on. They eventually arrived safe and sound into Abidjan. God's timing was perfect. On the next day the city was closed to all incoming traffic, forcing many people to spend the night at the roadside. God had His hand on the ladies in a marvellous way.

Ivory Coast was always considered to be one of the most stable countries in West Africa but that changed in December 1999. Since then the country has been plunged into war and bloodshed and is divided in two. The rebels largely control the northern part of the country while the government has control in the south. Missionaries and church friends are praying that peace will return again after the next elections.

During the years of political agitation the church in Ivory Coast has been through difficult times. The Church group with which UFM Worldwide is associated has churches in thirteen regions, ten of which are in rebel territory. Many have had to leave their homes, fleeing for their lives. Pastors were displaced and many of them have lost everything. However, through it all there have been tremendous testimonies to God's sustaining grace.

For the Browns and their missionary colleagues the political crisis in Ivory Coast, the subsequent war and evacuation from the country they love, subjected them to an emotional roller-coaster experience. There have been times, just when they thought the situation was settling down again, their hopes were dashed by another surge of violent combat. Back in Northern Ireland William and Rosalind wondered and prayed, *Will we get back?  When?  Where?*

The UFM Worldwide Council decided that the wisest course of action was for Rosalind and the children to return to Northern Ireland rather than William and Daniel trying to join them in Abidjan. Initially the family booked a one month return ticket Ivory Coast to Northern Ireland, thinking that everything would be resolved in a short time. However, God had other plans. Their stay at home lengthened out for almost two years.

Because of the unplanned stay in the United Kingdom William and Rosalind were able to fulfil a long held desire, to attend the CEF Leadership Training Institute in Kilchzimmer, Switzerland. The time spent in Switzerland equipped them with the much-needed training for children's work and the essential skills to train other children's workers.

Waiting is never easy! However, God is always faithful and in August 2004, God opened the door for them to return to the land to which He had called them. Because of the security situation they moved from the west to a more central and secure location, Yamoussoukro.

On their first Sunday back they had a time of fellowship with New Tribes Mission missionaries. The missionary who spoke that morning entitled his message, "A gospel worth dying for." The Lord reminded the Browns again of the tremendous privilege it is to take the gospel to lost men and women.

Before leaving for Africa William placed an order with EHC for the Children's Bible lessons in French. They look forward to making these available to put into the hands of hundreds of Sunday School teachers in Ivory Coast, both in the government held territory and in the Northern rebel held territory as this becomes possible.

William sent this report from Ivory Coast just a few weeks after they settled into the African way of life:

The ministry of EHC literature here in Ivory Coast has been invaluable. Gospels of John in French and booklets such as Christ is the Answer are continually much sought after. I always keep a good stock of John's gospels in my vehicle to distribute to soldiers at the numerous checkpoints. The people here are generally religious and many are searching for reality.

Just recently I was going through a checkpoint near a rebel held area. I gave the soldier a Gospel of John; he thanked me and then said "Pray that God will save me." Eternity will only reveal what has been accomplished through the ministry of EHC literature in Ivory Coast. Today these paper missionaries have gone to places where missionaries are not permitted to go because of the war.

As we look to the future we do not know how long we will be given to serve God in this land but we know that we are here in His will at the moment. The influence of Islam is growing stronger and is undoubtedly at the root of some of the political problems. Time may be running out and we want to make the best of the opportunities we have now to reach men and women, and boys and girls in Ivory Coast with the gospel, in word and in print.

We are waiting on the next container Samuel and Clive.

••••

Unexpectedly, William and Rosalind's plans were changed in November 2004 when old political wounds reopened and fresh fighting spread across the Ivory Coast. It was headlines all around the world. Bloodshed began when Ivory Coast warplanes killed nine French peacekeepers and an American aid worker in an air strike on the rebel-held north. France, Ivory Coast's former colonial ruler, wiped out the nation's airforce on the tarmac in retaliation, sparking massive anti-French rampages by mobs of thousands in the fiercely nationalist south.

In the middle of this unrest Rosalind sent out an urgent report at the end of October 2004:

Sadly things here in Ivory Coast are not really calming down. In Yamoussoukro we are blessed that our area is quiet, although we have not yet been able to venture into town as we have so far been advised against it due to anti white sentiment. The main businesses in town have been looted and most of the others are still closed. Today has been declared a day off in honour of the Muslim festival of Ramadam nearing its end so everything is closed today anyway. The feeling is that if the UN vote to press sanctions against Ivory Coast, as is very possible, then things will get worse.

Things in Abidjan are really heating up, and the main embassies are planning evacuation of their citizens from there. Even the French are planning to evacuate all who want to leave, which could be up to 8000 people according to the BBC. The British Ambassador telephoned us last night again, and told us to prepare to be evacuated if things do not calm down. He asked us to contact the French consul here in Yamoussoukro who would be responsible for any evacuation from here.

As a result of all the latest events the entire mission community here in our neighbourhood met this morning for a meeting at the school. We had actually started school at the time and the meeting was called at breaktime. The situation is such that ministry beyond the confines of our neighbourhood is impossible, while the school exists to support those who are ministering all over the country. There is no clear direction in the country at the moment, and no clear solution obvious either. There are so many factions now involved that it is all becoming a real mess.

School was suspended and we are all now at home. We don't yet know if there will be an evacuation from Yamoussoukro, but if there is it is unlikely that it will be by road as that is just not possible at the moment. We have to prepare to leave, while still hoping to stay and are trying to maintain some kind of routine and normality for the sake of the children. They also want to stay on here and cannot contemplate having to leave. They have been so happy here right from the beginning, and so have we. We have not talked to any of our Ivorian friends about this as we are just torn in two. The bombing on Saturday night was all the confirmation we needed to indicate that the situation could become very much worse and we have all been a bit jumpy ever since. In Yamoussoukro as a whole there are around seventy-two missionary personnel including children.

Some passages of scripture are very precious at the moment. Thank you to all who have written and encouraged us! Please continue to pray that the Lord will intervene in the situation and allow his work to continue here unhindered.

With widespread looting and continuing violence on the streets French and UN peacemakers took action. Twenty people were killed and over six hundred were injured. The situation was deteriorating quickly. As a result Rosalind sent another urgent report:

We have had another eventful day here. Daniel has had malaria since Tuesday and we were treating him for it with tablets but his temperature continued to rise and he was vomiting more and more last night. We telephoned the doctor and she prescribed a course of six injections instead, so William had to take him to the hospital twice today to have those. He will need four more over the following four mornings, but already the fever has gone and he has perked up considerably. William was wary driving into the centre of town, but apart from receiving a bit of verbal abuse from some youths he had no problem. Fortunately one of the New Tribes Mission missionaries is a nurse and is willing to continue the course of injections wherever.

Then today we got the news that the planned evacuation will take place tomorrow and the phone has been ringing all day. Between consuls, ambassadors and army generals of several nationalities, I think we've had a call today from everyone who is anyone in the region! We will be taken by British army plane from Yamoussoukro airport to Accra, Ghana. After much discussion they are taking all the nationalities on the same flight (around lunchtime) so the entire missionary community will be leaving together.

New Tribes Mission have had many meetings to discuss the situation here, and much prayer, and the general feeling is that the school exists to support the primary ministries amongst the Ivorian people, but in the present climate that sort of ministry has been curtailed, so the school is closing for the foreseeable future. We feel that the decision is wise. Please pray for safe travel to the airport which is just outside the town. We will have a military escort.

Thank you so much for all your prayer support for us. We have been conscious of a very tangible presence of the Lord and Daily Light this morning spoke right to us, "He led them on safely" (Psalm 78:53). Tonight when we prayed with the children we shared this verse with them, William asked the little ones three questions, "Who is He?" "Who are the 'them' in the verse?" and "What does 'safely' mean?" Cherith was straight in with, "He's God; 'them' -- that's us', and 'safely' means to be taken care of." They have been asking questions about what we are going to do and we have had to tell them we have no idea beyond tomorrow, but God is leading us on safely and that's all we need to know right now.

After finally arriving in Accra, capital of neighbouring Ghana, Rosalind was able to summarise the events and emotions of the previous few days:

The evacuation went smoothly. The Ivorian army provided us with a coach and an armed escort to Yamoussoukro airport on Friday morning. Colonel Philippe Mangou, who has just been promoted to Chief of Staff of the Ivorian army, planned that part of the evacuation. He was so kind, and told us that his father was a Methodist minister.

Pastor Koné, his wife and two other UEESO Pastors accompanied the party on the coach and sang choruses as we travelled. We were a total of 78 ex-pats from various countries, including 6 Jehovah's Witnesses! It was very difficult to say goodbye to the Koné family and friends and the tears flowed.

While we waited at the airport, French soldiers drove over from their nearby camp with bottled water and later with food rations. There was unconcealed mutual distrust between them and the Ivorian soldiers guarding the airport. The Sukoi jets were still sitting on the runway, with bits blown out of them from where they had been immobilised by the French army.

The French soldiers showed the children how to heat up the food rations using little flat packed stoves and that passed some time for the children. I even managed to make a greasy cup of tea by boiling water in one of the empty tins! A Canadian NTM missionary gave Daniel his malaria injection sitting outside the terminal building.

A Royal Air Force Hercules plane arrived with British soldiers on board and a young woman from the British diplomatic service. We got on the plane and since there were so many of us, we sat along the sides of the plane, or in the middle on top of our suitcases. There was hardly room to get between everyone. There was no air conditioning and we waited on the tarmac for a UN person who was supposed to come from Daloa. Eventually we were perspiring so much that we had to get off the plane and go back into the terminal. It was the first time we ever felt the cool air getting off a plane in Ivory Coast!

Finally we were all ready to go and after first being told that our luggage would not all fit and we could only take 15 kilos instead of the 20 kilos we had first been told, they then decided that since there were so many children it would all balance out. The soldiers were very kind, and there was a doctor and a nurse amongst them so Daniel got the very best of attention. One soldier sat down beside him on the floor of the plane and played noughts and crosses with him and kept losing, much to Daniel's delight. They also handed out British chocolate bars and took the children in small groups up into the cockpit to see the pilots and look out over the land. Matthew got chatting to the pilot and discovered he was from Ballymena!

We had very little heart for packing and didn't even use up 15 kilos allowance each, but just brought the bare essentials, letting the children each put their prized things in a small holdall. I chose what I thought were my strongest sandals, but between holding on for dear life as the plane took off and gripping to keep from falling over, they were broken by the time we arrived in Ghana!

The British army wasted no time, and the rear door of the plane was open long before we landed, giving us a nice breeze! We reckon it will be hard to listen to all the instructions that usually go with a commercial flight after this experience, with neither a seat nor seatbelt in sight!

The British High Commission staff were waiting to welcome us in Accra airport and did a tremendous job providing some debriefing and medical care not to mention sausage rolls, croissants, meat pies and chilled drinks and a play area set up for the children! They also provided a coach to take us all to our guesthouses.

We are presently staying at the WEC guesthouse here in Accra with a number of WEC colleagues who were evacuated with us. We are gradually trying to come to terms with the events of the past few days and have been going through debriefing sessions with the WEC West African Regional Director. Even though we are not WEC they have encouraged us to stay and take part in this and it has been very helpful. We had twenty people staying in a house with twelve beds, but one couple have now been housed elsewhere.  Some are moving on tomorrow, and in the next two days fifteen more WEC missionaries from Ivory Coast are due to arrive into Accra, so we may well be moving somewhere else soon.  There is also a debriefing session planned for the children in the next few days, which we feel will be very good for them.  It has also been good for them to spend these few days with some of their classmates, rather than having a sudden rupture of all their friendships.

We are still all in one room but it is bigger than the original one (now only two are sleeping on the floor)! and I think the children appreciate being together these days. (Even if Mum and Dad don't always appreciate it) We are slowly coming to terms with the events of the past couple of weeks. However when we hear the noise of aircraft flying overhead (like just a moment ago) we still feel a little 'jumpy' and await the explosion!

We would value prayer for guidance from the Lord for our next step. There are so many things to consider, including the children's education and we are just seeking God for His direction while at the same time recovering from the events of the past week.

In closing we want to share with you a comment made by sixteen-year-old Janelle, a pupil at Yamoussoukro International School on the same night as the bombing of the Ivorian military aircraft on Saturday 6th November. The children in the dormitory were very frightened. Later the same night Janelle said, "The Bible says 'As for God His way is perfect.' That means that what I am going through right now is perfect for me."

We take comfort from this as well knowing that God's ways are always perfect even though we don't understand them just now.

Wearing only light clothing and sandals William, Rosalind and the children arrived home at Belfast City Airport on Thursday 25th November 2004. Since settling into life again in County Fermanagh where the children have enrolled in local schools, William and Rosalind have taken up temporary roles as local representatives of Child Evangelism Fellowship for the West Tyrone area. They remain confident that God's way is always perfect and He will make their way perfect.

# 3

# FRED ORR AND THE PRECIOUS SEED

Several hundred people gathered into one of the largest auditoriums in Manaus, Amazonas in April 2004. Pastors of many churches across the evangelical spectrum, missionaries, both foreign and national, professors of local theological institutions and other academics were there to celebrate a special occasion and give thanks to God for the life and work of one person who had touched all of their lives. A special plaque to mark the occasion was presented to the guest of honour and veteran missionary, Fred Orr, upon completing fifty years of missionary service in Brazil.

The evening was not only a time for celebration for the long years of service. A flood of nostalgia filled the auditorium as speaker after speaker employed grandiose superlatives to describe Fred's work and ministry. Fred, who was becoming increasingly embarrassed and uneasy with each speech, was greatly relieved when an unexpected power cut prematurely brought proceedings to a halt and curtailed the number who might have paid tribute to this remarkable man.

Fred Orr began his life in the Castlereagh district of East Belfast. He and his wife Ina were members of Castlereagh Evangelical Church, now Castlereagh Baptist Church, where Mr. Willie McComb, former missionary to Brazil and founder of Acre Gospel Mission, was the pastor. Fred and Ina were converted to Christ as children. During their teenage years they only lived a stone's throw away from each other. Although Fred's chief pursuit as a young man was for football, at which he became very successful, it was only when he started to date Ina that he was drawn more into the fellowship at the church in Castlereagh.

After Fred and Ina were married in Castlereagh Evangelical Church they went to live at Knocknadonagh, just outside Lisburn. Although they moved out of Belfast, they still remained totally committed to the work of their home church. Ina and Fred both taught in Sunday school. Ina led the Junior Fellowship meeting while Fred was in charge of both the Intermediate and Senior Fellowships at the church.

It was during this time that Fred first met Ernie Allen who had just returned from the Bible College of Wales. Ernie had set up home in Omeath Street, on Belfast's Cregagh Road and was publishing Revival Movement booklets promoting revival. Fred was greatly impressed by the accounts of the various men God used to bring revival in former times. Neither man was aware then how their future ministries would help and complement the others'.

Fred was challenged about missionary work as a result of a special missionary offering. The Castlereagh Church had a "Young People's Missionary Society" of which Fred was chairman. This Society organized a Missionary Convention each year. Most of the children in the church had missionary boxes which were opened quarterly and the contents distributed to various Missions. After one of these box-openings it was decided to send a gift to the Worldwide Evangelisation Crusade (WEC) so Fred personally took a cheque to the WEC office in north Belfast. Mr. Willie Weir, the WEC secretary, was not at home when Fred arrived, but his wife, Mrs. Agnes Weir, attended the door and invited Fred to come in.

Fred explained to her the reason for his visit and reached her the cheque. Mrs. Weir did not even look at the amount on the cheque, but after thanking Fred she said, "What about you? What are you doing? You are young and strong. Why are you not on the mission field?"

Fred was taken completely by surprise. She then asked if Fred had ever read the life story of C. T. Studd, the Founder of WEC, to which he replied negatively. Mrs. Weir gave Fred a copy of this book and some other WEC magazines. This was the beginning of a process which led to Fred and Ina going to the WEC Missionary Training College in Glasgow in 1950.

Initially Fred and Ina, challenged by Andrew Lang's article in the WEC magazine, "World Conquest", felt the Lord was leading them to India. Although they were willing to go to India, yet through a series of circumstances and largely through the influence of Mollie Harvey, who was on furlough in 1952, the Lord definitely called the young couple to Brazil.

Both Fred and Ina were exceptionally gifted people. Ina's musical talents greatly complemented Fred's preaching and teaching ability. Both were engaged in evangelistic missions before embarking for Brazil. They also were gifted in children's work and conducted several children's missions. While still at the Bible College in Glasgow, a director of Child Evangelism Fellowship (CEF) approached Fred and Ina about the possibility of working with their agency. Although Fred declined the invitation he introduced the CEF director to Mr. Sam Doherty. Sam was a schoolteacher in Lurgan and he and his wife Sadie had been living with Fred and Ina in their home near Lisburn not long before this encounter. It was during that time at Fred and Ina's home that Sam and Sadie trusted the Saviour.

Sam and Sadie Doherty received the CEF director to their home during his visit to Northern Ireland, and subsequently, they accepted the challenge of pioneering the work of CEF in Ireland and then beyond to many parts of Europe.

On Sunday, 14th March 1954, there was a special farewell service for Fred and Ina at Castlereagh Evangelical Church. Willie McComb, the pastor, led the service. Fred gave a moving and challenging testimony of how God had unmistakably called them to Brazil. It was a memorable night, and those present never forgot how meaningfully Ina sang with great feeling what turned out to be almost prophetical words:

*O Lord this world is lost in sin,*
*So few there are who care,*
*Many of whom profess Thy name,*
*No burden will help to bear.*
*We need a passion Lord for souls*
*To bring the lost back to Thee,*
*Our hearts must be stirred*
*'Til all have heard,*
*At least once of Calvary*

*Let me burn out for Thee, dear Lord,*
*Burn and wear out for Thee.*
*Don't let me rust, or my life be,*
*A failure, my God, to Thee.*
*Take me and all I have, dear Lord,*
*And get me so close to Thee,*
*'Til I feel the throb*
*Of the great heart of God,*
*And my life burns out for Thee.*

Crowds were at the Belfast harbour on the following night to say farewell to a young couple who had so much to entice them to stay at home. However, God had called them and they painfully said good-bye to friends and family before sailing down Belfast Lough to the echo of hymn singing from the large company of well-wishers.

After visits to the exotic ports of Portugal, Madeira, Barbados and Trinidad, the SS Hilary finally entered the mouth of Brazil's mighty Amazon River. Fred and Ina's hearts were filled with joy for they felt that after five years of marriage and missionary training this was the land to which the Lord had brought them.

••••

When Fred and Ina arrived in Manaus six weeks after leaving Britain, they received a warm welcome from James and Dorrie Gunning and some American missionary friends. After James and Dorrie left for Ireland, the American missionaries, Willard and Grace Stull, took Fred and Ina on a tour of the various churches in Manaus, several of which had been founded by Willard. During the day, Fred attended to releasing their baggage from customs and trying to secure a place for themselves on the Catalina flight to Boca do Acre. At each meeting, Willard gave Fred an opportunity to speak while he interpreted for the congregation. He also tried coaxing Ina to sing, but she was reluctant to do so since she felt there was little point in singing in English when no one could understand her.

Fred and Ina did not want to be delayed in Manaus unnecessarily. They knew that Mollie was preparing for their arrival in Boca do Acre. Because no places were available on the plane, Fred and Ina decided to go to the Manaus port one Sunday afternoon to find out if there might be a boat heading to Boca do Acre or Labrea. Their search was not fruitless. They discovered a river steamer was leaving for Labrea in a few days and would take several weeks to reach Labrea. Eager to be on their way, the young couple decided they would travel on this steamer to Labrea. From there Fred and Ina planned to transfer to a flat bottomed paddle steamer that would take another week to reach Boca do Acre where Mollie and Jack and Joan Mawdsley awaited them.

On the night before they left Manaus, Ina finally conceded to sing at a meeting. She took the time to learn the Portuguese words of the hymn:

*The Name of Jesus is so sweet,*
*I love its music to repeat*
*It makes my joys full and complete,*
*The precious Name of Jesus.*

*"Jesus," Oh how sweet the Name*
*"Jesus," every day the same;*
*"Jesus," let all saints proclaim*
*Its worthy praise forever.*

Ina's voice penetrated into the night air like the voice of an angel and arrested the attention of many passers-by who stopped to listen. They came to the door of the church to gain a better view of this unknown singer. Even a passing "bus," which was only a converted lorry used to transport people to town, stopped outside the church and let the passengers listen to the young missionary singing. They were not aware that this would be the last time Ina would ever sing for the Saviour on earth. Appropriately, she expressed her purpose of being in Brazil as she sang the last stanza of the hymn,

> *No word of man can ever tell*
> *How sweet the Name I love so well*
> *Oh, let its praises ever swell*
> *Oh, praise the Name of Jesus.*

Fred and Ina had never seen anything like it. Even as Ina sang and before Fred spoke, people came to the front of the church to accept the Lord Jesus as Saviour. During those days in Manaus the couple had not only won souls for Jesus Christ, but had also gained many friends in Manaus.

The next evening they arrived at the boat that was to transport them up river. Many of the believers came to bid farewell to the missionary couple at the floating harbour where the boat was moored. The believers sang to them and presented Fred and Ina a heart-shaped cake that was beautifully decorated as an expression of their love for the young couple they had come to know so recently.

Fred and Ina were glad to leave Manaus even though they had thoroughly enjoyed the time spent with Willard and Grace. They felt their place was further in the interior where many had not yet heard the gospel of the Lord Jesus.

The boat was small but the captain had given Fred and Ina a cabin on the steamer's upper deck. He also insisted that they eat their meals with him. Although they could not understand what he was saying, they appreciated his kindness and sat with him at each meal, smiling at his complimentary comments.

The meals consisted mostly of meat, rice, beans and manioc followed by a dessert of bananas and thick jam made from guavas. Fred and Ina ate most of what was set before them without too much inquiry about what they were eating. However, Fred was careful to avoid drinking river water for fear of falling victim to typhoid or dysentery, which was so prevalent in the area. He insisted on them only drinking bottles of soft minerals, and Ina even cleaned her teeth with the famed Amazonian soft drink, Guarana.

After six days of travel, Fred and Ina were sitting at the table having another meal with the steamer's kind captain. It was Saturday about 6.00 p.m.. During the course of the meal Ina realised that she had eaten a piece of offensive meat. Too embarrassed to remove the foul bite she decided to swallow it. Fred was aware and preoccupied that Ina had eaten the foul meat but made no more comments about it.

They completed their meal and retired for the evening to their tiny cabin. During the night, the steamer continued to make its slow progress upstream. The next morning they had their customary breakfast with the captain.

On Sunday afternoon, even though it was hot and humid, Ina said to Fred, "I feel cold."

Fred put a thermometer below Ina's tongue. The mercury mark read 104°. Both suspected the fever was the result of the bad meat Ina had eaten the previous day. As he held on to the thermometer, Fred had a strange premonition that this fever was more than just a passing chill. *Is God taking Ina?* He asked in the quietness of his heart. *Don't even think that way*, he chided himself. He prayed but had no real assurance that God was going to heal Ina.

On the boat, there were very few medicines, but Fred gave Ina some aspirin to try to help sweat the fever out of her system. Ina had little or no appetite but took small sips of the bottled Guarana.

The high temperature persisted even though she had no pain. Fred felt helpless to alleviate Ina's plight. The steamer was taking them farther up river every day, and it seemed that they were getting farther and farther away from any help. Fred held Ina's hand and prayed that the Lord would touch her. Still, the fever raged. Together they quoted the promises God had given them and reaffirmed their commitment to God's call on their lives and their love for each other.

Each day they travelled farther into what was commonly known as the "Green Hell," and Fred could not help wonder why all this should be happening to them. The captain and his crew became increasingly very anxious for the well being of their young passenger, but because of the language barrier they were confined to expressing their feelings by making gestures with their hands to encourage Fred. It was frustrating not being able to communicate orally. The captain tried to tell Fred that there might be help in Labrea, a town a few days up river from Canutama.

Even though Ina was very ill and the fever continued to rage, she had no sense of alarm or fear. At times she chided Fred for showing anxiety and doubt. There was little sleep for either of them. Their waking hours were spent conversing, reminiscing, reading the scriptures and praying.

On the following Thursday the slow moving steamer finally arrived in Labrea, which was located on a sharp bend of the river. To everyone's surprise and relief, they discovered there was a doctor in Labrea just as the captain had said there might be. Hopes were raised when the doctor was brought to the steamer to see what he could do for the lady missionary.

Sadly, it was already too late. Ina grew weaker during the afternoon. Fred never left her side. On Friday morning she called Fred, who was trying to mask his real feelings of doubt and fear. Try as he would, he could not hide these real feelings from Ina. After Fred prayed he looked straight up into her face as she said, "Now that's the Fred I know. You go and get on with the work and I am going to have a little sleep."

Those were Ina's last and very significant words. Ina fell asleep in Christ at eight o'clock that evening, Friday, 4th June 1954. She was only twenty-nine years of age and had been in Brazil for just over six weeks.

A thousand thoughts filled Fred's mind as he sat in his cabin in the early hours of Saturday morning. He thought of Ina's mother back in Belfast who just a short time earlier had lost her husband. He thought of his parents and their anxious thoughts about him. Besides the family, there were also their friends at the Castlereagh Church and a myriad of other friends at home.

While thoughts crowded in on Fred's mind, he felt constrained to read his Bible even though he was in a spin of confusion. In the back of his mind was the haunting question, "Why did God allow her to die if He has called us out here?"

At times it seemed as if the Devil whispered to him, "You should never have come out here."

Fred was not in the habit of opening his Bible at random and looking for a verse. However, he still cannot recollect how he got his Bible open to John 13. Immediately, Fred's eyes fell on the page of his Bible and it seemed that verse seven stood out in large bold letters right across the page, **"Jesus answered and said unto him, What I do thou knowest not now; but thou shalt know hereafter."**

The words shook Fred. He looked back and could not see the verse again in such bold letters. He had to search to find that the quotation was in John 13:7. This word was the voice of God to His child and gave Fred the great assurance and peace that he needed in the midst of his frustration and heartbreak.

Not long after Ina's death Fred wrote to Willie McComb, pastor of the Castlereagh Church and secretary of Acre Gospel Mission, and in his letter, he disclosed a measure of the grace God gave to him under the extremely trying circumstances.

Loving greetings in the precious name of Jesus! Just a few lines to let you know that I am keeping well and finding His grace sufficient for each day. I am sure it was a terrible shock to you to receive the news of Ina's home-call. It all seems like a wild dream, and I feel I shall awake from it. At such a time as this one is inclined to ask, "Why?" but we must trust in

Him, who never makes a mistake, and seek to glorify His name in it.

I am sure you realise something of the burden upon my heart, and I ask that you would pray and influence others to pray also at this time. How many things seem to add up in these days and throw light upon mysteries of the past! I do not just say this as Ina's husband, but truly, God used her mightily, right from Belfast.

On board the ship she won the hearts of all, and I have seen big men stand at the rail and cry as she testified for Jesus and then sang His praises. The places we called at and the witness she bore there, especially in Brazil, the Lord knows. The greatest of all her witness was in Manaus, and then on the boat to Acre. The believers just loved her, and I have seen the church as well as the road outside packed, as she sang for Jesus. Many people told me that she sang beautifully in Portuguese. Grace Stull suggested that she should record some hymns, since there are very few hymns recorded in Portuguese.

I had letters from Grace and Willard Stull in Manaus today. They say that when Ina's name is mentioned in the church, there is hardly a dry eye. The other evening, the evangelist in Willard's church asked the people to rise and observe a moment's silence in honour of Ina. Afterwards they sang "Whiter than the snow," which was one of the last pieces Ina sang there.

On the boat she again won many hearts, including that of the captain, who was a real father to us both. We spent hours on the bridge with him, and we lacked for nothing.

Never once did Ina complain. She was actually running over with joy. She would say to me, "Freddie, why are you afraid? Don't you trust the Lord?" She was an inspiration to me and even made me kneel at her bed to confess my sin of doubting, and ask for faith to trust in Him. This was early in the morning of the very day she went home.

Right from the start she had no pain, and as far as I know, she had none right until the end. She became delirious on Friday afternoon, and then went unconscious about 6.00 p.m. and passed away two hours later.

God alone knows what a week I spent, as Ina slept very little and I sat with her right until the end. The Lord seemed to be preparing me for what lay ahead, for I could not get the thought out of my mind right from the start. Ina's condition did not do this of itself, for as I have already said, she never seemed to be seriously ill. Her temperature was very high, although one day it was almost normal again. She actually sat on deck for a few hours on two occasions, though the second time she had to go back to bed because she felt a little queer.

The doctor took a blood slide and said that there was no sign of malaria. She went so quickly that it is hard to believe, especially since she was in the best of health previously. Even the doctor said that she was very strong, yet in six days, she was gone.

Thank God, He is still my trust. To Him be all the glory. The way before looks dark, but I feel that He who called us to serve Him has all the answers. Ina never doubted her call and was emphatic that she was where He would have her, even during her sickness.

This was a sacrifice of monumental proportions. In almost all of Fred's correspondence to this day, he heads the letter with 2 Corinthians 9:8; "God is able to make all grace abound toward you; that ye, always having all sufficiency in all things, may abound to every good work." He most certainly would be justified in endorsing this verse with the words, "tried and proved to be true."

Some time later, recollecting on the events of Ina's final days and how God spoke to and sustained him, Fred wrote these appropriate words:

*I cannot always understand*
*The way God works His mighty plan,*
*But this I know, His love to me*
*Is deeper than the deepest sea and*
*Some day soon His face I'll see,*
*And then His promise unto me*
*Will be made real, I'll understand*
*And praise Him for His guiding hand.*

*He drew me out of nature's night,*
*And o'er my pathway shed His light.*
*I've walked with Him the narrow road*
*That leads my spirit up to God and*
*Some day soon His face I'll see,*
*And then His promise unto me*
*Will be made real, I'll understand*
*And praise Him for His guiding hand.*

*So by His grace I'll follow on*
*To know the Lord, God's blessed Son.*
*My glory shall be in His cross,*
*For which I count all else but loss and*
*Some day soon His face I'll see,*
*And then His promise unto me*
*Will be made real, I'll understand*
*And praise Him for His guiding hand.*

••••

Fred caught a flight to Boca do Acre where he was cared for during those difficult days by Mollie Harvey. In spite of his horrendous experience Fred decided to apply himself to study and master the Portuguese language. This was not only good therapy for him, but also his focus paid worthwhile dividends. Very soon, he was speaking Portuguese exceptionally well and began to take part in various meetings. The people at the Boca do Acre loved him, and being aware of his circumstances, they sought to express their sympathy and support.

Even though he had vowed never to return to Labrea which held such dark memories, he felt he should return to erect some kind of memorial at Ina's grave. On arrival in Labrea, Fred did not know where to go. There were no hotels and Spanish priests and nuns dominated the town. However, as Fred walked up to the bank an old lady recognised him and said, "You are the Englishman that lost his wife here a few months ago?"

By this time Fred could understand some Portuguese, and he nodded his head in agreement with the lady. She continued, "Would you like to go to the cemetery?" After a visit to the graveside Fred was still not sure where he was going to stay, so he returned to the boat which was not leaving until the next day.

Early the next morning, he ventured up to the town again and met a tall gaunt man with a short beard. His name was Alfredo David, a Syrian trader who had made his home in Labrea and ran a shop just at the corner of the town square. Obviously recognising who Fred was, he inquired of his well-being. During the course of their conversation Fred told him he would love to find a place to stay in the town. The Syrian said that Labrea was no place for a man like Fred and recommended he should go elsewhere. "This place has too many sad memories for you," He pointed across the town square to the Bishop's large residence and said, "and what is more they will put you out."

Fred insisted that he would like to stay but was not sure where he could find a place. The old man disappeared into the back of his shop and called on his son, Alfredinho, to open a store a few doors up from the shop and make room for Fred to stay. The young boy duly complied and swung a hammock across the room for the stranger in town.

The store was completely overrun with rats, which sometimes fell into the hammock where Fred was sleeping. There were no toilet facilities whatsoever. When it got dark, he had the use of a little tin lamp which gave a dull amber light but also filled the room with smoke. However, the smoke was not strong enough to deter the mosquitoes which came in their droves to feed on fresh Irish blood. This was the first foothold in Labrea and proved to be the Lord's provision.

When the mayor of the town saw the conditions in which Fred was staying, he was greatly embarrassed and offered Fred a piece of land on which to erect a house. At the town hall, he gave Fred the deeds of the land after Fred had paid the stamp duty, making Fred the legal owner. However, the Bishop was so powerful in Labrea that he not only overturned the legal document Fred had acquired for the land, he also had the mayor sacked from office and deported out of Labrea.

Fred stayed long enough to erect a headstone at Ina's grave and then returned to Boca do Acre. A lawyer friend in Boca do Acre learned that the Bishop in Labrea had taken land which had been given to Fred and offered to pursue the matter further. Fred graciously declined the offer, preferring to let the Lord work it all out.

Within a few months Fred ventured on another visit to Labrea, constrained that the Lord had a work for him to do there. On arrival, he found that there was a lot of local sympathy for how he had been treated by the Bishop on his previous visit. In the outpouring of this emotion, Sr. Alfredo David offered to sell Fred a piece of land. Fred was grateful for the man's kind offer, knowing how much this old Syrian cared for him, but he did not have the wherewithal to buy any land.

Without betraying his complete lack of funds, Fred said he would look at the various sites the man offered. Fred did not have enough money to buy even the worst site, but he felt he might as well ask how much the best site would cost. Alfredo David told Fred to go ahead and fix a house on the site and they would talk about money later. Rather than be caught out on a shortage of funds later, Fred insisted on knowing the price right away. The man urged Fred to secure the land, as he was in no hurry for money.

When news of the Syrian's offer to Fred leaked, the Bishop was furious. He contacted the judge in town and through him sent word to Alfredo David, urging him to go ahead and sell the land to the foreign missionary. The Bishop would then use his influence to dispossess Fred and give the land back to its original owner. When Alfredo David heard of this, he was angry at the conniving Bishop and refused to cooperate. The Bishop continued to press the matter further and told the town councillors to impound all the property the Syrian owned in an attempt to frustrate any missionary incursion in Labrea.

The saga continued to and fro for several months while Fred returned to Boca do Acre to await the arrival of James and Dorrie just before Christmas in 1955. Meanwhile, the judge fell in love with the Syrian's daughter and somehow was persuaded to see things from her father's point of view. Consequently, he refused to follow the Bishop's edict. The Syrian eventually became the judge's father-in-law. The judge then advised Sr. Alfredo David to let Fred use the land but retain his own name on the documentation. In so doing, it would secure the land for all parties concerned.

Fred and James, and later with the help of Allen Loney, built a house on the land which not only provided accommodation for the missionaries, but also had a wide verandah on which they conducted meetings.

For the next twenty years Fred remained in Labrea until the church called its own pastor. During those Labrea years, not only was a church founded, Fred was in demand for conferences and evangelistic campaigns in other parts of Brazil. Through travelling to these other regions Fred caught the vision of teaching and training Brazilians for the work of the ministry.

On 1st February 1969 Fred married Zeni Batista de Souza in Manaus. Zeni was a graduate of the Regular Baptist Seminary in Manaus. God blessed their home with two children, Fred and Florence. After several years in Labrea the family moved to Manaus where Fred pursued his vision of training Brazilian workers. A Tuesday night Bible school was established, and several workers joined Fred to set up the Cruzada Amazonica, an agency set up to train workers and reach out in evangelism.

Melquides, one of the young men studying with the Cruzada on Tuesday evenings, led a team of other students to distribute tracts and booklets at the local port.   Small boats and ocean liners came to dock in Manaus, and this was a strategic opportunity to present the gospel to all who arrived and departed from there.   During those days there were several outstanding conversions of people who returned to their own distant locations to be witnesses for Jesus Christ.

One of the early acquisitions for the Cruzada was a property for a Christian bookstore in the centre of Manaus. Besides becoming the principal centre for distribution of Bibles and Child Evangelism Fellowship material, the Cruzada also was a centre for distribution of gospel literature for the whole of the Amazon.

During various visits to Northern Ireland Fred renewed his acquaintance with his friend Ernie Allen and was amazed at the way God had been blessing and enlarging the work of the Revival Movement. At Ernie's invitation, Fred agreed to speak at various conferences which Ernie had organised for the newly formed, Every Home Crusade (EHC).  Fred challenged Ernie and his small staff about preparing literature in Portuguese for use in the Amazon.

That was the beginning of a close relationship between the Cruzada Amazonica and EHC.  Initially small packets containing hundreds of gospel tracts and thin gospel booklets were sent through the post to Fred's postal address.  As the demand for the literature grew, EHC in Belfast prepared tea-chests full of The Way of Salvation booklets and A3 size posters with the Bible texts; "Jesus saith unto him, I am the way, the truth, and the life: no man cometh unto the Father, but by me" (John 14:6).  "For there is one God, and one mediator between God and men, the man Christ Jesus; Who gave himself a ransom for all" (1 Tim. 2:5-6).

Tens of thousands of these posters were circulated to pastors and evangelists all over the Amazon.  The pastors and evangelists in turn distributed the literature to thousands of people who lived in remote parts of the Amazon region.  For years missionaries reported that when they visited simple forest homes in the most remote regions and distant tributaries it was not uncommon to find several of the EHC posters pasted to the interior walls.

EHC not only provided the literature, they undertook to pay the transport and any import duty on the literature. Sadly the customs procedure in Manaus became increasingly complicated and expensive. Providentially, another missionary in Brazil, Victor Cardoo, who was working with Christian Literature Crusade (CLC), offered to take responsibility to receive the EHC literature in 18-tonne containers in São Paulo and then circulate it to missionaries all over Brazil.

This arrangement was excellent. São Paulo was more central for reaching Brazil's 160 million population, nearer to the great cities and offered a less cumbersome procedure for importation. The friends at the Cruzada Amazonica continued to receive large quantities of EHC literature and use it effectively in their outreach ministry. They also taught pastors and evangelists the value of the printed material and how to use it.

While all this evangelistic work continued Fred was challenged to concentrate his efforts to plant a new church in a heavily populated but much neglected district of Manaus. Although this new venture had a small beginning with children in a garage, it quickly developed into a flourishing church, the Igreja Evangelica de Hebrom (Hebron Evangelical Church). Missionaries and local Christians used the EHC booklets to help evangelise the whole district. Every home in the area received the booklet, "The Way of Salvation."

After acquiring a property in the same district, renovating and extending the building to keep pace with the growth of the work, they finally built a new church while still preserving the original structure at its core. The building today is the home of Hebron Evangelical Church. Fred's Tuesday Bible Study developed into the early beginnings of the Hebron Bible Institute, which was also housed at the Hebron Evangelical Church building. Young men and women enrolled at the Hebron Institute for missionary and pastoral training in other regions of Brazil.

When CLC ceased to operate in Brazil, Victor Cardoo no longer had facilities to handle EHC containers of literature in the Portuguese language for Brazil, South America's largest country. However, several Brazilian evangelists and pastors in the south of Brazil offered to become agents to distribute the literature to missions and missionaries for EHC.

The Hebron Bible Institute was upgraded to the Hebron Theological Seminary with more than forty students and their own premises at the former headquarters of Acre Gospel Mission. One of the principal features of the evangelism course is the use of good gospel literature as provided by EHC. Today, like the flowing of the waters of the Amazon, a steady stream of gospel literature flows from the EHC factory in Belfast, reaching earth's remotest regions and quenching the spiritual thirst of thousands with the gospel of Jesus Christ.

One of Fred's favourite Bible texts summing up his fifty years in Brazil is Psalm 126:6, "He that goeth forth and weepeth, bearing precious seed, shall doubtless come again with rejoicing, bringing his sheaves with him." Fred shares the firm belief with EHC that the "precious seed" is the Word of God and like his friend Ernie Allen, during these fifty years, through preaching and the printed page, he has given his life to hold forth the Word of Life.

# 4

# A GREAT DOOR INTO INDIA
## *Tom Orr*

Pastor Tom Orr from Belfast and Tom Lewis, British Director of BEE International, were a little weary after the long flight from the United Kingdom, but they were also spirited with eager anticipation to meet their Indian friends at Hyderabad airport. This was their first visit to India, and when they emerged from the KLM airliner and entered the arrival terminal they were taken aback. They were totally unprepared for what awaited them and could never have anticipated the warm and lavish reception prepared for them. Not only was there a sea of happy and ecstatic people to greet them, but a large banner elevated above the crowd spelled out "WELCOME". Both men emerged from the restricted baggage area and were received with colourful garlands of flowers which were placed around their necks while Pastor Jona Savarapu and his wife Vijaya welcomed them with the traditional Indian courtesy followed by a warm embrace.

Tom Lewis had travelled in Asia on many previous occasions, and this was not Tom Orr's first visit to the Asian sub-continent. He was quite overwhelmed by the warmth and love of Jona's reception. Even in the middle of all the fanfare Tom could not help thinking how marvellously God had worked to make all this possible.

Tom was born and reared on a farm just outside the village of Crossgar, County Down. He loved the farm and even after completing his education he still continued to work the land on the family's holding.  His parents were religious upright folk though not evangelical. They strictly observed the Sabbath and everything that related to the church but had little time for evangelism and evangelists. While Tom was still a boy the family changed residence from their proximity to Crossgar to another farm nearer to Downpatrick

When Tom's brother was converted at W. P. Nicholson's Tent Mission in Downpatrick in 1938 Mr. & Mrs. Orr did not take kindly to their son responding to the preaching of this well-known, outspoken and unconventional preacher.  However, their disapproval could not deter God working in their family.  Further displeasure came to the home four years later when their other son Tom also made his decision to receive Jesus Christ as personal Saviour.  Some years later this displeasure was alleviated when Tom led his mother to personal faith in Jesus Christ and received her into membership at Killyleagh Baptist Church.

July 12 is a celebrated day for most Ulster residents, but this same date has a deeper and more significant meaning for Tom Orr.  That was the date of Tom's conversion.  Having been influenced and impressed by the change in his brother's life, Tom was searching for satisfaction and peace in his life. Although he attended the family church regularly he had never heard the gospel preached there. One Sunday afternoon when he returned from the farmyard he picked up a gospel tract that someone had left in the house.  It was the title that drew Tom's attention, "The Christian and Amusements" written by Australian evangelist Dr.. Peter Wolffe. Tom's quest for truth seemed to find an answer in Dr. Wolffe's message, and in the privacy of his own room he prayed for forgiveness and salvation.

Although Tom's conversion also incurred some resentment in the family, it was not so severe as that experienced by his brother. Nevertheless, Tom had made his decision to follow the Lord Jesus Christ. Through his late teens he continued to grow and develop in his Christian witness and became an avid reader of the scriptures. His decision to leave the family church to worship at Killyleagh Baptist Church was not welcomed at home, but it became a milestone in Tom's life.

At Killyleagh Tom became fully involved in the work of the church and was active in open-air evangelism and tract distribution. Mr. Tom McNabb, pastor at Killyleagh Baptist Church, took a great personal interest in Tom. Pastor McNabb not only invited Tom to speak at the church prayer meetings but also arranged for him to conduct meetings at mission halls in that part of County Down. So impressed was Pastor McNabb with the potential shown in Tom Orr that he encouraged him to consider pastoral ministry. Tom declined Pastor McNabb's advice due to severe migraine headaches which he frequently suffered, nevertheless, the pastor persisted in his endeavours to encourage Tom into deeper Bible study by introducing him to Dr. Graham Scroggie's Bible Study Course. While Tom was still farming he embarked on this course and committed himself to it for four years.

During those four years Tom came to a crossroads in his life. His father died and left the family farm to be divided between Tom and his brother. Since the brother was immigrating to Australia it became necessary to sell the holding. In this crisis Tom earnestly sought God's will for his life. At first he pondered on the possibility of buying another farm, but declined this option after some inquiries. He also applied for a job in the Ministry of Agriculture but was unsuccessful because he was deemed to be too young for the position.

Soon Pastor Thomas Seawright replaced Tom McNabb at Killyleagh Baptist Church, and young Tom Orr continued to his give faithful service to the church. However, Pastor Seawright's pastorate was short and unexpectedly interrupted when he accepted an invitation to become pastor of a church in Bradford, England.

The pastor's departure corresponded with the crisis in Tom Orr's life. Tom's good friend, David Kennedy, an elder at the Killyleagh Baptist Church, not only bought the family farm, but he voiced his opinion to the church members that Tom Orr would be a suitable replacement to fill the pastoral vacancy. The result of David's perception and recommendation resulted in a unanimous call from the church for Tom to become their full-time pastor. Having tried all other doors Tom was convinced this was the Lord's leading for his life. Tom was twenty-two years old when he commenced his ministry in Killyleagh Baptist Church.

Tom settled in to his new position with much dedication. God had given His servant a word that had been commanded to Elijah the prophet more than two thousand years earlier, "Go hide thyself." That is what Tom did. Every morning from 7.00 a.m. until noon he devoted to the study of the scriptures, theology and church history. He believed in being properly equipped for handling the Word of Truth.

Right from the beginning God blessed Tom's ministry. Numbers began to increase and he had a good group of young people around him. Two years after becoming pastor, Tom married Mary Taylor who was also a member of the Killyleagh Church. God blessed their home with a son and a daughter.

The membership at Killyleagh doubled in number under Tom's ministry, but Tom considered his thirty years as pastor in Killyleagh as his building years. During those three decades various churches approached Tom about the possibility of accepting an invitation to become pastor of other churches. Tom gave due consideration to each of these approaches, but never felt any liberty to move away from Killyleagh.

It was during the holiday season in 1978 that Tom received invitations to preach at two Belfast Churches; Shankill Baptist Church and Rathcoole Baptist Church. He didn't feel at liberty to dismiss these requests. He went to Shankill Baptist for a Sunday and followed this with two Wednesday night Bible Studies. The Secretary of Shankill Baptist, Mr. John Hawthorne, asked Tom if he would allow his name to go forward as a candidate to fill the pastoral vacancy at the church. Following Tom's consent to John Hawthorne's request, a unanimous call came from the congregation, and Tom began his ministry in Shankill Baptist Church in December 1978.

Life in the heart of the Shankill Road in busy Belfast was a complete contrast to that in the quiet rural village of Killyleagh on the edge of Strangford Lough. Some people thought Tom had taken leave of his senses to accept a position on the Shankill Road after thirty years ministry in Killyleagh.  After all, this was 1978 and "the troubles" were at their worst in the city. The "Shankill Butchers" had gained infamy, and the city was scourged with daily bombings, murders and kidnappings.  Nevertheless, Tom was sure that God had called him to this work, and he had no hesitation in accepting the challenge.

For nine years Tom continued his ministry in Shankill Baptist Church, and during this time God greatly blessed and used His servant. In those years many people were converted, a large number of new members were added to the church and an Annual Missionary Convention was established.  However, late into his ministry at Shankill Baptist, Eric Cameron from Rathcoole Baptist Church approached Tom to help at their midweek Bible Studies.  For three winters Tom conducted these Bible studies every Monday night.  The numbers began to grow until there were well over a hundred people attending these meetings.  Furthermore, all the studies were recorded, and a large tape ministry was established which circulated Tom's ministry to many distant parts of the world.

The visiting ministry to the Bible Study at Rathcoole eventually led to Tom finally accepting a call to pastor the Rathcoole Baptist Church in 1987.  Again Tom's preaching and pastoral ministry was greatly blessed by God. Very soon the church was well filled, many were saved and many were added to the church and an annual missionary Convention was established which continues to this day. It was also during this time that Tom was invited by Tom Lewis to become Chairman of the Board for BEE International UK.  This increased Tom Orr's interest in missionary enterprise even more.

One day in 1997 Tom received a telephone call from Mrs. Edith Morrison, a retired Christian teacher who was a member of nearby Abbott's Cross Congregational Church requesting a visit from Tom. During their conversation Edith told Tom about her ongoing support for Jona Savarapu, a full-time Christian worker with what was to become known as the United Grace Mission in Hyderabad, India. Knowing that Tom had quite an extensive audio-tape ministry, Edith asked if she might have permission to send his tapes to her friend Jona in India. Tom was only too glad to grant the request.

In the months that followed Tom furnished Jona with more new material for his Bible ministry in Hyderabad. Little by little Tom was increasingly drawn into the work of the United Grace Mission. He later discovered to his great delight that Jona had preached one of Tom's sermons fifteen times. Jona apologised for his "plagiarism" without prior permission. Tom was only happy to learn that the sermon, "Tell Jesus", based on John 12:12, had been of such use to Jona in God's work

Jona was reared in a Christian home in India but as a young man he rebelled against his family values and left home. He travelled to India's east coast where he found employment as a shipping clerk. However, Jona was not able to escape from God's Spirit.

One day while Jona was reading a copy of the Bible in a remote part of the country, an Indian Christian man noticed and read to Jona from Luke chapter 16, the story of the rich man and Lazarus the beggar. After reading the chapter the man urged Jona to make a decision -- either he could choose Christ and be ready for heaven, or choose the way of the rich man, and like him, go to hell. It was an opportune moment, and Jona accepted Jesus Christ.

Like the prodigal son returning to his father, Jona headed home soon after his conversion. He felt he would have to fulfil the Indian custom for a son and care for his ageing parents. His father however, urged Jona to serve God spreading the good news of salvation instead of caring for them.

Jona spent the next five years pursuing a pastoral course at a Baptist college in Madras where he gained a Bachelor of Theology degree. During the college course Jona acted as a translator for visiting speakers at the college, and this opened the door for him to assume some leadership among the students. After graduation Jona taught in two Bible Colleges and pastored an English-speaking church for two years.

When Jona and his wife, Vijaya, went to Hyderabad in 1986 in obedience to God's call, they had almost no possessions. Jona had a vision and burden to establish a work that would reach the multitudes on the streets of Hyderabad, a city of more than four million people. Life in the city was exceedingly difficult. The young couple had no home. At night Jona slept under a tree after he found a room somewhere for Vijaya. For three months they walked the streets of this vast city, searching for an opening to begin God's work. Nothing seemed to emerge.

Initially it was hard to get the work started, and Jona became increasingly distressed thinking he might have missed God's call in some way. However, a very special moment of divine affirmation was just around the corner. One day while Jona was walking down a busy street he stopped at a second-hand bookstall. As he browsed through the volumes his eye fell on a magazine entitled "The Flame", a publication of the Church of the Nazarene. No one knows how the magazine found its way to a bookstall in Southern India.

In the magazine Jona noted an advertisement which offered free Christian tracts for use in evangelism. Keen to find tools to help in his outreach, Jona thought, This is what I need. He noticed the address. It was that of Mrs. Edith Morrison, Abbey Park, Doagh Road, Newtownabbey, Northern Ireland. Jona not only requested a supply of tracts, he also asked Mrs. Morrison for permission to translate her tracts into the local language of Telegu.

After Edith Morrison eventually received Jona's letter she sent her reply to a Post Office Box as he had indicated. However, in the meantime, circumstances had forced Jona to close the PO Box. Although the letter arrived in Hyderabad, Jona did not obtain it. Convinced that the connection between himself and his potential benefactor in Northern Ireland would not materialise, Jona watched the months go by.

A year later, he went back to the post office with the intention of taking out a new box number. The official in charge objected, saying that there was much demand for the box numbers and that none were free. Jona persisted and eventually he was allocated the very same box he had given up a year earlier. When he opened the box he discovered Mrs. Morrison's letter which had safely lain there for a whole year.

By this time Jona had erected a very plain building to house the United Grace Mission and although the work began to grow it was not without opposition. On one occasion a Hindu fanatic called at the door and asked to see Jona. When another member of the church went to the door instead, the fanatic stabbed him with a knife. Through God's grace Jona and his friend both survived, but the would-be assassin paid for his crimes when he died of a stab wound within a year of his assault on Jona.

For his first Sunday in his unpretentious church hall Jona had a congregation of one. On the second Sunday, there were six people. Notwithstanding the slow beginning, within a year, God had blessed the United Grace Mission, and over sixty people were attending the services. Today one hundred and fifty people attend the services in this place.

Because of Edith Morrison, Tom was able to make a contact with Jona and the exchange of correspondence resulted in Jona inviting Tom to visit India for preaching seminars. Tom's first visit to India was with his close friend, Tom Lewis, and was originally planned for March 1998 but arrangements had to be changed. The collapse of the Indian government early in 1998 and the civil unrest which followed made it unsafe to travel. Tom postponed their trip until November that same year when Jona indicated that it was safe to travel.

Tom gave an account of that first trip:

"On Sunday we travelled to Visakhapatam and then set off for Pasavadala for what Jona had advertised as a "Good News Festival". This Hindu town was usually four hours' journey away by car, but the recent torrential rain had turned the road into a pot-holed disaster area! It was fully eight hours before we arrived. We went to bed immediately as we had to be up early the next morning in order to take the Bible classes which had been organised in two daytime sessions, lasting two hours each.

We were amazed to find that Jona had contacted so many pastors and Christian leaders from all across this part of Andhra Pradesh State. Days of prayer and a great deal of visitation had been undertaken, and now a great number were here to sit under our ministry.

The evening meetings were devoted to the preaching of the gospel of Jesus Christ. Each meeting was three hours in length and the numbers gradually increased from three hundred at our first service to a thousand by the end of the week. Thankfully there was no opposition to our ministry and indeed there was much interest throughout the town. Later visits to India would prove how fruitful the visit had been in the growth of new churches in the area.

It was while sitting on the platform one night in Pasavadala, that God gave me a vision of a yearly convention in Andhra Pradesh State, when the good news of the gospel might be preached and believers taught from the scriptures. This is a vision that is now, I am glad to say, materialising.

We headed back towards the large seaport of Visakhapatam on the banks of the Bay of Bengal, and there we experienced quite unforgettable scenes both during and after our ministry to the people. I shall never forget one middle-aged lady who came up to us on the platform and prostrated herself at full length, throwing her arms around my feet. Crying out repeatedly in Telegu, she said that she was a sinner. Then she turned to Tom Lewis and with a similar prostration of herself, called out "Oh, Jesus, take me to heaven." Clearly, God's Spirit was working in her heart in a most effectual way. Having made a profession, she turned up at the pastor's house, on the next day, and greeted us.

Two hundred and twenty-five Christian leaders and pastors came to the Bible readings, and hundreds of people responded to the call of Christ at the evening meetings. When we finally left the cry "return, return" echoed in our ears."

In November 1999 Tom Orr and Tom Lewis visited India again where they conducted Good News Festivals in Samalkot and Pasavadala. During this trip the itinerant evangelists saw over 2,200 men and women respond to the message of salvation.

During these visits Tom was able to use Every Home Crusade (EHC) literature which was sent out from Belfast. Tom's letter was published in the EHC newsletter in February 1999:

On the 21st November 1998 we arrived in India for special meetings, arranged by Pastor Jona Savarapu. The first series of meetings were held out in the villages. The second series in the city of Vishakapanam on India's east coast. The meetings were held each day from 9.30 a.m. until 12.30 p.m. then from 2.30 p.m. until 5.30 p.m. and from 7.30 p.m. through to 10.30 p.m.

The ministry combined both the teaching and preaching of the Word of God. During these "Good News Festivals" many hundreds of people attended. Two hundred and twenty-five Pastors gathered for ten Bible readings and evening meetings. Hundreds of souls professed faith in Christ. We are grateful to Every Home Crusade for forwarding 10,000 copies of the Gospel of John and 20,000 copies of the "Way of Salvation" in Telegu to help with this work. The Spirit of God is moving in this land. There is a mighty harvest being gathered in India.

Tom undertook further trips to India in successive years with Pastors Lawrence Kennedy, Evan Williams and Geoffrey Ward accompanying him on separate journeys. Good News Festivals were organised for various centres, and some times up to 3,000 people attended these events. During the Festival all students are provided with a notebook, a pen, and a small rosette with each individual's name inscribed upon it. Hospitality and refreshments are also provided for the period of the festival. God has provided for all these needs.

Tom again wrote of the work of Every Home Crusade helping in this gospel outreach and training of Indian pastors and evangelists:

Every Home Crusade, whose work was established by Ernest Allen in Belfast some years ago, has proven to be a big help with Christian reading material. Literature is translated into Telegu and delivered to the thousands of Indians whom the United Grace Mission contacts each year. In 2001, the first year in which the Every Home Crusade was heavily involved in our work, some 30,000 copies of each of the following three booklets were translated and printed in Belfast and sent out to India to await our arrival in January 2000, *A Gospel of John, The Way of Salvation* and *Pardon and Assurance.*

Also of value to us are the small decision cards. On each card is a space for the name, address and vital details of the individual. The cards also have room to note whether the decision made at the gospel service indicated a profession of salvation or of restoration. These cards have proved invaluable as they enable the local pastors to engage in precise follow-up work.

There were many testimonies to grace that touched my heart on my third trip to India. One man said to Lawrence Kennedy, 'I am fifty-six years old and never in my life have I had opportunity for teaching such as this.'

Perhaps one of the most memorable individual testimonies to the power of the gospel was that of an elderly man whom we met one day, in a little village at the far end of a secluded laneway. As we sat on his verandah, he told us how he had heard the gospel through the labours of a missionary, several years ago. He read a Bible and was converted, taking his public stand for Jesus Christ soon after. In due course, some men came to the door and, putting a knife to his throat, said "Renounce Christ, or we will kill you." Although they did not come back to fatally harm him, much persecution followed. Thousands of people, mainly Hindus, come under the gospel, and hundreds respond at the end of each meeting. In Samalakot for example, 5,000 people were present, with about 400 persons responding to the gospel invitation each evening. The copies of the Gospel of John in Telegu were invaluable and were given to those who waited behind to profess faith in Christ. The remainder of the Gospels will be used in door to door work in what is a predominantly Hindu place. I have no doubt a great harvest of souls has been reaped and will continue to be reaped in time to come.

Jona was able to visit Northern Ireland in 2001. He had never been out of India before. During his visits to a wide range of churches and halls, Jona stirred the imaginations of all who heard him speak, especially when referring to those villages where he had recently engaged in visitation work. People had said to Jona in these places, "Who is this Jesus?" Jona shared with the Christians how he had a vision to put evangelists into these hitherto unreached areas.

During his visit to Northern Ireland he was able to make a visit to Mrs. Edith Morrison's grave. Edith had passed away six months before Jona arrived. Although he had never met this lady he felt he owed so much to her.

Tom reported on another development of the work of the United Grace Mission.

A Christian brother in Ireland came to visit me in Carrickfergus with the particular spiritual burden that he wanted to finance the erection of a new church building somewhere in India. Such an opportunity was immediately seen as an answer to prayer in the ministry of brother Jona. Now a strong brick building is in place which can hold one hundred and twenty people. Once again, God's providence has been at work, both in Ireland and in India, as the United Grace Mission continues to grow.

As one looks back over the story of The United Grace Mission it is amazing to trace God's sovereign hand in it all; through Edith Morrison's relationship with Jona Savarapu and the story and development of the Good News Festivals, one cannot help being overcome with joy and wonder. We can only bow the knee and worship.

More recently twenty-five local evangelists have been added and placed on the field, and they are carrying out some of the new work spoken of by Jona on his visit to Ireland in 2001. Some evangelists are sponsored by believers in Northern Ireland, and in that way the work has become very precious to the heart of many Ulster Christians.

Seven large church buildings and several smaller buildings have now been erected where new congregations have been founded.

India is the world's largest democracy with a population of more than a billion; more than a quarter of these are under twenty-five years of age. United Grace Mission is now reaching into 560 villages with 140 workers under the leadership of Jona Savarapu. Jona leaves home every Tuesday morning or evening and does not return until Saturday or Sunday morning when he gives his weekly ministry report to the church. During these travels he visits the churches and spends time with each evangelist to encourage, help and counsel. Almost every week he baptises ten to twenty-five new converts.

The UGM also maintains the orphanage with eighty-one children accommodated in the home in Hyderabad. These children are a mixture of orphans and semi-orphans. Trading in orphans is something forbidden by Indian law, but alas such trading is carried on. At the orphanage all the children are not only provided with an education, but also are taught the scriptures daily. Twenty-five severely handicapped children are cared for in the Jonathan Boyd Hostel which is designed to provide care for such children

Early in 2005, 7th January, six other friends, Pastors David Legge and Lawrence Kennedy, John and Grace Boyd, John Wade and Sydney Johnston, accompanied Tom for the seventh UGM Festival in Southern India. Numbers exceeded anything he had seen in previous years. At the first centre up to ten thousand attended the evangelistic crusade each night. Many hundreds responded to the gospel message at the end of each meeting. At the second centre, located in a larger town, up to twenty thousand people were attracted to the festival each evening with multitudes spontaneously responding to the call of the gospel. This huge response from anxious souls required a large amount of gospel literature which was supplied by Every Home Crusade. The EHC also provided "Creation to Christ" lessons for use among the pastors who attended the various seminars.

Tom concludes this survey of UGM's work:

> Every penny contributed, every tract printed, every vehicle given, as well as the ongoing work amongst the churches and pastors' seminars, is bearing much fruit for the Lord and yielding a mighty harvest. May that Holy Name be magnified through UGM, both here and in the United Kingdom.
>
> Let me personally close with the thought that India is the second largest nation in the world, its economy is swiftly growing, and its political stability is more assured than at any time in recent years due to a new more moderate government. Unparalleled opportunity therefore is before us. Let us hear this "Wake-up" call that a harvest in this land is ready to be reaped.
>
> My thanks are now due to all who are the hidden force behind the work, praying, sharing and giving. My thanks are also due to my fellow board members for their time and concern for the work. My appreciation is due to Every Home Crusade for the many thousands of Gospel of John, tracts and teaching materials for children's work. The Child Evangelism

Fellowship must be thanked for thousands of teaching kits for children's work. I am also grateful to Mr. and Mrs. Balmer from Belfast who have supplied vast amounts of George Goodman material to encourage the pastors and evangelists.

The opportunity for mission in South India is being grasped; we are working where no witness has existed in certain places within living memory. The privilege is ours of telling the gospel of Christ for the very first time. Let us awake to the call; all we are and all we have been, we owe to Christ. All we ever will be, we owe to Him. Evangelism, combined with the literature of Every Home Crusade, will cause a lasting work to be done in India for the Lord. Let us all then join together in service and in bringing glory to our Lord and Saviour, Jesus Christ.

My personal thanks go to Every Home Crusade for their contribution to the work of United Grace Mission. We are deeply indebted to all their workers at the factory in Belfast. Through their literature we have been able to evanglise many villages, confirm and fortify the faith of many young believers and supply literature to numerous Indian evangelists who are zealous to spread the gospel of the Lord Jesus Christ.

Tom is already planning to return to India and has requested more EHC literature to use in the Christian festivals organised by Pastor Jona and the friends of United Grace Mission.

# 5

## SOWING THE PRECIOUS SEED
### *with*
### *Pixie Moles (Nee Caldwell)*

The War in Europe arrived on the doorstep of Northern Ireland in 1941. Wave after wave of German Luftwaffe aircraft screamed overhead in the night skies over Belfast. They dropped their deadly cargo of bombs in a random blitz of the city in a vain attempt to paralyse the strategic and valiant efforts of the workers at Harland & Wolffe Shipyard. The conflict was real.

As a result of those dreadful nights of the Belfast blitz many local people became more keenly aware of just how grim and frightening the European conflict was. They even feared the possibility that their own beloved land could be invaded by Nazi armed forces.

It was during that dark time that young Pixie Caldwell was first challenged by another conflict. Her father had taken her to missionary rallies at Belfast's Wellington Hall. There she heard missionaries reporting on the spiritual conflict in reaching men and women with the gospel in the distant continents of Africa and Asia. These missionaries spoke of millions held by evil superstitions and suffering from grim sicknesses such as leprosy and malaria. They also reported the triumphs of the gospel in hitherto heathen hearts. The missionary reports challenged Pixie's heart and their words stimulated her to read the great missionary biographies of men and women who had hazarded their lives in service for Christ. Unknown to Pixie, God had His hand on her young life and was shaping her for similar service in years to come.

It all began with her conversion to Jesus Christ in 1938. Her parents had always made sure that their four children, a boy and three girls, attended church and Sunday School. Mr. & Mrs. Caldwell were God-fearing people. Mr. Caldwell did not enjoy good health and on several occasions was so seriously ill that there seemed little hope of recovery. The thought of death provoked Pixie to think a lot about eternity and the reality of heaven and hell.

Every February the Young People's Convention in the Wellington Hall in Belfast's city centre, attracted large crowds. Pixie was only twelve years old when she attended the schoolgirls' afternoon rally. At that rally she responded to the gospel message and after the meeting she prayed with one of the leaders and received the Lord Jesus as her personal Saviour.

When she returned home, she wrote the words of John 3:16 in the flyleaf of her Bible, making a slight but meaningful alteration: "God so loved me that He gave His only begotten Son that if I believe in Him I will not perish but will have everlasting life". Writing out these words gave Pixie full assurance of salvation and filled her heart with peace and joy.

Soon after claiming the promise of eternal life in John 3:16, she was challenged by the last command of Christ in Mark 16:15, "Go ye into all the world and preach the gospel to every creature." She often wondered how any young man or woman who had health and strength could fail to obey Christ's command when millions as yet had never heard the gospel message. Before leaving Bloomfield Collegiate

School, Pixie was doing the Senior Certificate French Oral Exam, when she told the examiner that one day she hoped to be a missionary in China.

At this time, however, Pixie had very little experience of the Christian's need for continual fellowship with the Lord Jesus through prayer and personal Bible study. Soon after arrival at Queen's University, at a Bible Union Conference, she was greatly helped by an address on the Holy Spirit. The visiting speaker advised the students to buy a book by Dr. Andrew Murray; *Abide in Christ.*

Pixie shared the book with her mother, and soon the promises of John 15 became precious to them both. They began to pray together and to encourage each other in the Lord. Mrs. Caldwell continued to read the book, often a chapter daily, until her last illness, and then Pixie read it to her.

World War II ended during Pixie's course at Queen's and members of the armed forces began to return home, including her only brother. However, this other and deeper conflict was not over. It was the spiritual battle against the powers of darkness in heathen lands. There was also a conflict in Pixie's heart at the time of her graduation and during the time she was teaching at Victoria College in Belfast. As she read about those people who were unreached by the gospel in West Africa, she became very burdened by their need, but sadly Pixie was also beginning to count the cost of missionary service overseas. As she read the Scriptures she continued to hear the resounding call of Christ in Mark 16:15; "And he said unto them, Go ye into all the world, and preach the gospel to every creature."

Jesus' promise in Mark 10:29,30 was also a constant challenge to her waiting heart; "Verily I say unto you, There is no man that hath left house, or brethren, or sisters, or father, or mother, or wife, or children, or lands, for my sake, and the gospel's, but he shall receive an hundredfold now in this time, houses, and brethren, and sisters, and mothers, and children, and lands, with persecutions; and in the world to come eternal life."

One night God spoke very clearly in a vivid dream. Pixie still recalls it quite distinctly:

In the dream I arrived in heaven, and stood before a great multitude all robed in white, row upon row, as in a vast arena. Sorrow instead of joy filled my heart. My life had ended and I had not gone to West Africa. Someone was standing beside me, an angel, I thought.

"Are there many from West Africa here?" I asked him.

"Very few," he replied as he pointed to a group in the multitude. "Many have been called by God to take the gospel to them and have married and stayed at home."

He concluded by quoting Paul's letter to the Romans 10:14 "How then shall they call on Him in whom they have not believed? and how shall they believe in Him of whom they have not heard? and how shall they hear without a preacher?"

In spite of the confirmation of God's call in this dream, Pixie still recalls with shame that she was slow to obey. At that time it was difficult for her to sing this challenging hymn at missionary meetings:

*I can hear my Saviour calling,*
*Take thy cross and follow me.*

After some inner struggle, peace only came at last with full surrender to the will of God. Again she could sincerely pray in the words of the hymn she loved:

*Where He leads me I will follow,*
*I'll go with Him, with Him all the way.*

Two years were spent at Ridgelands Bible College in Kent, now amalgamated with All Nations' Christian College. The students had a lovely motto; "The love of Christ constrains us" (2 Corinthians 5:14). For her own life's motto Pixie added three words from the following verse in 2 Corinthians 5:15 so that it read, "The love of Christ constrains us, Henceforth unto Him."

In 1952 Pixie sailed to Nigeria with the Sudan United Mission, (now Action Partners' Ministries, allied to the International Mission

Pioneers). A month before she left home, her father told her that forty years earlier he had heard God's call to go as a missionary to Nigeria. He was sad that he had not obeyed this call, but overjoyed that his daughter was chosen of God to go to the same land. Mr. Caldwell visited Pixie in Nigeria for several months during 1954-1955 and had the opportunity to lead some Nigerians to the Saviour. In 1964, on the morning God called him home, he gave a moving testimony to his fellow patients that he had the joy of speaking to Africans about the Lord Jesus.

During her first years in Nigeria Pixie's main work was in a Mission Boarding School, teaching boys who came from pagan and animistic tribes. Those students who surrendered to Christ soon wanted to share the gospel with others. "Many are learning to read in our towns and villages," they said, "and there are few Bibles. We need Scripture tracts in English, Hausa, Tiv, Ibo and Yoruba, to distribute during our school holidays."

Pixie reported on the wonderful way in which God supplied the need:

A few days before the end of term God gave me a promise from Isaiah 32:20, "Blessed are ye that sow beside all waters." The vision became clear. God was calling the students to distribute the written Word in distant towns and villages, but where could hundreds of Scripture tracts be found? I had just a small bundle. I felt it was like that lad's five loaves and two fishes. Several days later two large boxes of tracts were miraculously brought to my house. They arrived just in time for the students to take them to their villages. I was reminded of what Hudson Taylor said "God's work done in God's way will never lack His supply."

In 1964 Pixie returned to Newcastle for furlough soon after her father's home-call. Among his personal belongings she found a few Every Home Crusade tracts, and booklets on revival. As it was usually very difficult to obtain many Christian tracts in Nigeria, Pixie wrote to Every Home Crusade to request a modest supply to pack in her baggage for her return to Africa. Pixie had never heard of Mr. Ernie Allen, so this was her first contact with him. Mr. Allen replied promptly and told Pixie that the leaders of EHC had been praying for an open door for literature overseas. This was God's answer.

Through that door which opened in 1965, thousands of Scripture leaflets and booklets began to enter Africa. The first literature was in English, later in 1985 literature followed in the Hausa language and then in the Nigerian and Cameroonian Fulfulde also. Those who prayed for this open door could never have imagined that the floodgates of blessing have been unlocked in answer to their prayers. Huge containers of literature have been travelling by sea and land to Nigeria, to Cameroon and to Ghana.

The first English tracts were used in the schools, mainly by four enterprising ex-students who started tract distribution centres in four parts of Nigeria. During the Biafran War of 1966 many soldiers expressed gratitude for the help received from these tracts. A few years ago one of these ex-students resigned from his university lecturing post to engage in full-time evangelism with Gospel Unlimited, an evangelistic outreach to Muslims which he founded.

> Most of the literature from Every Home Crusade has been received by Christians and seekers from pagan tribes. In answer to prayer more and more Muslims of the Hausa, Fulani and Kanuri tribes have been obtaining it too, especially in Christian hospitals and clinics. Those who have openly witnessed for Christ have always faced opposition, and most have had to flee from their homes.
>
> In recent years militant Muslims have burnt down large numbers of churches in Northern Nigeria and have killed several thousand Christians, most of whom came from pagan tribes. In spite of this opposition, more and more Muslims are eager to hear and read the gospel message.

Pixie began to visit Fulani homes while teaching in a Mission School. Ten years before her retirement God called her to full-time evangelistic work with Nigerian Christians. The Lord gave her a vision that He was calling Christians from pagan tribes to visit the Fulani and all Muslim homes "two by two", and they were to go fearlessly as "lambs among wolves" (Luke 10:1-3).

The Fulani tribe is still considered largely unreached. There are almost thirty million Fulanis in Africa, but few of these have ever heard the gospel. They live among other tribes in sixteen countries of North West Africa; some are political leaders in Nigeria and Cameroon, some wealthy businessmen, but most are cattle rearers. Nearly all Fulani Christians have had to flee their villages and communities and the majority are too afraid to return home with the gospel message.

In one of the first Fulani homes Pixie visited, she explained the gospel message from the Wordless Book with its black, red, white and gold pages. That day a little girl began to believe the story of the cross of the Lord Jesus. Today she is one of a small number of Fulani Christian women. After she was treated and recovered her health in a Mission Hospital, her parents gave her to Pixie and in this way she escaped persecution.

In Northern Nigeria, as in many Muslim lands, Christian literature can rarely be distributed openly. Often in a market place or village, Pixie would hear a whisper in the Hausa language from behind or from her side, "Have you any tracts?"

The folded leaflet would be quickly and furtively put into an outstretched hand. One night while Pixie returned home in her car, a group of Fulani lads emerged from behind a bush. Their faces were illuminated by the headlights of the vehicle. Early fears were soon allayed when the young men requested gospel literature. Twenty minutes earlier they had seen Pixie in their home, but were afraid to reveal their interest in the gospel as an older brother was watching them.

Pixie is convinced that in many Fulani homes there are anxious sheep seeking the Shepherd among the rabid 'wolves'. Pixie remembered the night she shared the gospel message with Fulani women in their hut after a meal of maize porridge.

Outside, Fulani men, young and old were eavesdropping. Soon through the low doorway many hands were grasping for Scripture booklets I was using. I could not see their faces which were concealed in the darkness, just their hands by the light of a bush lamp. As I returned home with a Nigerian friend that night, over a rocky road, I pondered. *Would the seed of the written Word bear fruit?*

Two years later, during a return visit to Nigeria a Fulani man arrived at my door. "You have never seen my face," he said. "You just saw our hands the night you gave us the Scripture booklets through the low doorway. When I read the booklet, I believed the gospel. Later, a Christian passed by in my workplace and saw me reading it. He helped me to understand the gospel."

For me it was just like the story of the Ethiopian eunuch in Acts 8. Providentially, the Christian who passed by the friend's work place was a pastor. Sadly, Abe, the Fulani believer, is afraid to witness at this time because soon after he became a Christian his house was burnt down. His nephew, Bi, however, is witnessing openly to Fulani. He also received a Scripture booklet through the doorway, and later fled from his home in order to be free to follow the Saviour.

"Even if they kill me," he told us recently, "I will be happy because I will see the face of Jesus."

Those who witness to migrating Fulani people seldom ever meet the same people again. The migrants make long journeys on foot in search of pasture for their cattle. Pixie will never forget the Fulani father who asked her for a tract:

A long trail of Fulani with their cattle suddenly appeared on the horizon. Soon they would disappear. I stopped the car and ran towards them. "Safe journey," I called as I ran towards them. As I drew nearer I continued, "I have an important message for you about the way to heaven."

"Tell our father. He is behind," replied the young men controlling the cattle. I greeted the women and children as they passed. Some were borne along by slow moving oxen. Then came father. To my surprise, after a short greeting he asked in the Hausa language "Have you any tracts?"

As I took out my only tract from my handbag, he drew out a tiny cellophane bag from his breast pocket, then folded the tract and carefully put it inside. A second or two later he was off in pursuit of the cattle trail. I marvelled that even these migrating Fulani respected our Christian literature and the tiny clean bag was ready to receive God's Word. I had no doubt that his heart too was ready to receive the good Seed.

The question of a migrating Fulani mother will always be remembered by Pixie Moles:

As I told the story of the Saviour and His cross, the mother stirred the porridge in a tiny pot over a flickering fire.

"Did He die last week?" she asked. "Did you hear it on the radio?"

As we said good bye to that little Fulani family, the father, mother and baby were preparing to spend the night under the stars. We could only commit them to the Good Shepherd who had said "Behold I, even I will both search my sheep and find them out" (Ezekiel 34:11-12).

The EHC tract *The Broad and Narrow Way*, with its illustration of the cross at the entrance of the Narrow Way to heaven, has been given to countless thousands of Muslims in Nigeria, in the English, Hausa, Fulfulde and Kanuri languages, and has also been distributed widely in Northern Cameroon. Pixie recalls using the tract on a visit to Cameroon with a Fulani pastor from Nigeria:

I can still see the young Fulani mother in the Mission Clinic looking intently at the picture tract *The Broad and Narrow*

*Way*. "I can't understand," she exclaimed in Fulfulde.

A little later as the story of the cross was repeated; "I understand a little," she said.

When Pastor John explained it all again the young woman joyfully cried out "Now I understand."

As I looked at her I thought of the old hymn, *Tell me the story simply that I may take it in.* We were not able to accompany the mother and son to their distant home near the Sahara, but she left with the EHC tract in her bag and God's Word in her heart.

While Pixie was visiting refugees for a short time in London, she showed the picture of *The Broad and Narrow Way* to a Kurdish family. A young girl of twelve or thirteen looked intently at the picture, then jumped up from her seat between her parents. She fell to her knees and pointed to the Cross and cried as she asked with deep emotion, "Did you see it happen?"

The question asked by the Apostle Paul 2,000 years ago is still pertinent, "How shall they hear without a preacher?"

In her memoirs Mary Slessor wrote, "My life has been one long daily record of answered prayer for physical health, for mental overstrain, for guidance marvellously given, for dangers averted, for enmity to the gospel subdued and for food provided." Pixie wrote these words of Mary Slessor in her prayer notebook as a reminder of God's faithfulness. Pixie didn't endure the same hardships or face danger from cruel and primitive tribes as did the famous pioneer, but she praises God nonetheless for His protection, His leading and especially in her outreach to Muslims. She also proved God's faithfulness in practical ways. Pixie didn't find it easy to drive on the hazardous roads, yet she travelled thousands of miles without accident and is even glad that any punctures always seemed to occur near her home.

It is now over fifty years since Pixie went to Nigeria and over forty years since God gave her the promise from Isaiah 32:20 "Blessed are ye that sow beside all waters." She has found the promise to be especially poignant when they sing the following song at Every Home Crusade conferences:

*Blessed is the service of our Lord and King,*
*Precious are the jewels we may help to bring,*
*Down the passing ages words of counsel ring,*
*He that winneth souls is wise.*

*Out upon the highway, going forth with prayer,*
*For the lost and straying seeking ev'rywhere,*
*Close beside the Shepherd, we His joy may share,*
*He that winneth souls is wise.*

In 2003 Pixie married a former missionary with Action Partners' Ministries, Dr. George Moles. George and Pixie maintain an active interest in the Mission's work in Nigeria and the continuing effective outreach of Every Home Crusade.

After forty years, Every Home Crusade is still one of the main sources of gospel literature in three main language groups in Nigeria, English, Hausa and Fulfulde. Reports continue to come from evangelists, pastors and missionaries of God's blessing on the printed page.

Pixie never ceases to praise God that she found a bundle of Every Home Crusade and Revival Movement tracts and booklets among her father's documents.

# 6

## THE GOSPEL AT THE GATEWAY
### *Hazel Miskimmin*

It was a balmy evening in July 1961 when several hundred people gathered near the water's edge where the black water of the River Lagan blends into Belfast Lough. The spirited crowd was there to sing their favourite gospel songs as the old Liverpool Boat loosed its moorings and pulled out of Donegall Quay. From the side of the departing ship three missionaries waved enthusiastically to their family and friends on the quayside while many astonished passengers looked on. The crowd on the quayside responded with loud and ecstatic strains of the appropriate hymns for such occasions; "God be with you 'til we meet again" and "Take the name of Jesus with you". The singing wafted across the water and echoed off the surrounding buildings. The handkerchief-waving crowd remained vigilant and in jubilant song until the vessel drifted down the Lough and the sight of their missionary friends slowly receded from their view.

Missionaries James and Dorrie Gunning, who were returning for their third term in Brazil, were accompanied by the latest recruit for the Acre Gospel Mission's work in the Amazon, a nurse called Hazel Miskimmin. All three were greatly encouraged by the fond farewell from the many friends who had taken time to come and sing them on their way. With the company now out of sight, James, Dorrie and Hazel busied themselves along the boat's narrow gangways to find their respective cabins for the overnight crossing of the Irish Sea.

James and Dorrie soon found their accommodation, and when Hazel finally found her sleeping compartment she discovered another lady was already there to share the two-berth cabin. After exchanging pleasantries, the lady remarked, "There must be some important people on the boat tonight to have had such a big crowd at the quayside to see them off."

Hazel was a little embarrassed but never one for losing an opportunity to witness for her Lord, she volunteered, "Important people indeed. Our supporters came down to see us off. We are on the King's business and are taking the gospel of the Lord Jesus Christ to distant Brazil." That set the tone for the ensuing conversation, and Hazel took the opportunity to give testimony of what the Lord Jesus had done in her life.

Hazel was the eldest of Johnny and Annie Miskimmin's four children. Like her brother and two sisters, her childhood years were greatly influenced by her parents, several Christian aunts and their dedicated Sunday School teachers who keenly taught them the simple truths of the gospel. During the Second World War and before her sisters were born, Hazel and her brother Jackie were evacuated with their parents to Kells, a small town near Ballymena. It later seemed quite appropriate that Hazel spent those war years near to the old school house where the Ulster Revival of 1859 had its beginning. It was also there that a Christian schoolteacher not only gave them a good educational grounding but also spent time teaching his pupils the Word of God and showed concern for their spiritual welfare.

At the end of World War II the family returned to their home at Arkwright Street, between the Crumlin and Shankill Road in Belfast.

After several years absence from the city and having been greatly affected by life in the rural area of County Antrim, young Hazel with her rosy-red cheeks found it strange to adapt to city life in Belfast's narrow streets again.

Hazel was able to pick up the friendships which, to her thinking, had been inexplicably ruptured several years earlier. One girl whom Hazel hadn't seen since they were both only three years old, became her closest friend and the two girls were almost inseparable. They really enjoyed each other's company at school and in play. After the family returned to Arkwright Street the Miskimmin home was blessed with two more daughters. They were a delight to young Hazel who loved to fuss over them and care for them.

As young teenagers Hazel and her friend were often invited to various gospel meetings which were frequently conducted in the many mission halls in the area. In October 1947 a mutual friend of the two girls had been converted at an evangelistic campaign in the recently opened Keswick Street Mission Hall and was very keen to bring others to know the Saviour.

As often happens in most friendships, Hazel and her best friend had some differences and parted company for a few weeks. However, a few days later a young boy arrived at Hazel's door with a small piece of crumpled paper in his hand. He was the brother of Hazel's estranged friend. When Hazel opened the piece of paper she read the note. It was from her friend who suggested that they both go together to a meeting in Keswick Street Mission Hall.

Hazel was delighted to make amends and accepted the invitation. Keswick Street Mission Hall was located in a building that had once been a wine shop but lay vacant for a considerable time. Joe Anderson, a Christian in the community, owned a home bakery in Tennant Street, and with the encouragement of a few Christian friends he decided to rent the unused premises for reaching friends and neighbours with the gospel. The venture resulted in Keswick Street Mission becoming Joe's life investment.

When Hazel and her friend arrived at the renovated wine shop they were surprised to find it was packed to capacity. With some effort they were able to find a place and soon settled down to enjoy and take part in the enthusiastic singing.  Eventually a tall, thin preacher emerged from a little prayer room at the side of the platform and took his place near the reading desk with Joe Anderson. The preacher stood up after a brief introduction and bellowed out his welcome to all present.  His loud voice nearly made the girls jump out of their seats for they were almost within touching distance of the platform.  The Reverend Ian Paisley was the young evangelist, and he was conducting his first gospel Mission. The girls soon got used to his loud but resonant voice as they sat up and paid attention to what he had to say.

The preacher read his text twice over, "He, that being often reproved hardeneth his neck, shall suddenly be destroyed, and that without remedy" (Proverbs 29:1). Like a carefully aimed arrow the text went straight into young Hazel Miskimmin's heart.  "Often reproved…hardening his neck". That summed her up and it seemed as though the sword of the Spirit had pierced her soul. Hazel's mind travelled back to her aunts, and all their genuine care for her spiritual welfare. Hazel also recalled the challenging gospel messages that she had heard during her childhood. At those times she felt she would have liked to be saved, but she decided to put it off until a later occasion.

Hazel cannot recall all that the preacher said that night, but she was aware that he repeated John 3:16 several times.  This made her young mind think back to the times when, as a very young child, she was made to stand on a table or a chair while visiting her grandmother Miskimmin's home and asked to recite that verse as her party piece for all the family, "For God so loved the world that he gave his only begotten Son…"

As the meeting drew to a close, Rev. Paisley pleaded with those present who had hardened hearts to repent and come to Christ.  In the final appeal of the meeting the preacher called for those who had heard God's voice to respond.  Hazel struggled in a personal and mental battle. God had given her a vision of Calvary and of the Saviour's love for her, and she desperately wanted to respond to His love, but she also felt the pull of the world.  It was a dilemma for the young girl.  She was afraid that she was in danger of hardening her heart. As Hazel reasoned these matters she was distracted by a sense of activity beside her. She opened one eye, to find that her friend had already stood up indicating her desire to receive Jesus Christ as Saviour. That was just the encouragement Hazel needed, and in an instant she also rose from her seat to stand beside her friend.

After the meeting the two friends sat side by side in the little prayer room as the Reverend Ian Paisley read a number of Scripture texts to them. They each prayed a simple prayer asking forgiveness for their sins and accepting Jesus Christ as their Saviour. That was on Friday, 27th October 1947. Hazel Miskimmin was only fifteen years old. Little did she know then that the decision she made that night would have far reaching consequences in directing the course of her life.

Mr. & Mrs. Miskimmin were overjoyed with the news of Hazel's conversion even though they had not yet received the Lord Jesus as Saviour. Hazel's aunts were delighted for this answer to their prayers. They could not have anticipated what was yet to come.

Before the end of that year Hazel was challenged for the first time about the possibility of serving the Lord in a full-time capacity. A group of Americans visited the Albert Hall Mission on the Shankill Road to conduct a Christmas service. Hazel and some more of her new Christian friends went to hear the team. They thoroughly enjoyed the evening, but at the end of the service one of the team leaders asked a very direct question, "If the Lord should call you to serve Him as a missionary in some foreign land, would you be ready and willing to go?" Those words hit home, and the challenge touched Hazel's soul.

Since her conversion, Hazel had shown great spiritual enthusiasm and was very keen to serve the Lord. She felt she was ready to do anything and willing to go anywhere for her new Master. However, the reality of it was a sobering challenge, and when Hazel began to consider all that was involved in going to a mission field she began to have second thoughts. Hazel knew that it might entail leaving the security and warmth of a loving family and leaving all her friends.

Hazel felt that she wasn't yet ready to take that step. She was content to serve God locally and continue with her normal life.

Another obstacle that dampened her enthusiasm of going into missionary service was the thought of having to go to Bible College to train for the mission field. Hazel had never been particularly fond of school. Against her parents' wishes she withdrew from her business-training course at Belfast Mercantile College and started a job at the Faulat Shirt Company in Agnes Street. The prospect of returning to full-time study did not inspire her. In fact, Hazel was sure she was anything but ready or willing to go to some distant mission field. She preferred just to stay at home.

In the few years that followed her conversion, Hazel continued to enjoy and develop in her Christian life. She had so many like-minded friends who enjoyed attending youth rallies and Faith Mission conferences. They were having a great time in Christian fellowship. Ironically, the very enjoyment of these activities closed Hazel's mind to the challenge of missionary work. She tried to avoid reading Romans 12, which speaks of "presenting your body a living sacrifice, wholly acceptable unto God." However, try as she did, there was no way of escaping the call of God.

Hazel was confronted with a very forcible challenge during an evangelistic mission at Keswick Street. Evangelist Johnny Cupples was invited to speak at the Saturday evening Youth Fellowship where he presented a great missionary appeal from the Word of God. At the conclusion of the meeting the evangelist asked for a show of hands from those who would be willing to go and serve the Lord on the mission field, should God call.

In spite of a prolonged invitation no one responded. Hazel felt miserable as she remained in her seat. She really wanted to be of some use to God but wasn't prepared to surrender her all to the Lord Jesus.

After the Youth Fellowship a good number of the young people congregated in a friend's house. One of the ladies present, a neighbour of their hostess and a member of the Keswick Street Mission, said something that startled all present. "See you young people," she stormed, "I was ashamed of the whole lot of you tonight! There wasn't even one of you interested in serving God!"

Some made excuses while others remained silent. Hazel was among the silent ones, but she smarted with pain in her heart as her conscience worked overtime. To try to appease her conscience she decided to pledge her generous financial support to some foreign missions and missionaries, reasoning that if she could not go to the mission field herself, then she would at least support those who did.

During the Easter weekend in 1953 Hazel attended the Faith Mission Convention in Hamilton Road Presbyterian Church, Bangor as she had done for several previous years. She was almost twenty-one years old. Dr. Alan Redpath was the speaker at the convention, and his theme was titled "One Hundred Per Cent For God."

Hazel was intrigued to hear this well-known and respected man of God confess in the course of the meetings that he had once heard the call of God on his life to go and witness to "China's millions" but had failed to obey that call. Now he reckoned that what he was doing was only God's "second-best". The thought of a "second-best" Christian existence frightened Hazel. She wanted to know the best in her life and give the best to her Lord. Hazel, therefore, felt that she ought to yield her best to the Saviour and surrender her all to Jesus Christ.

At the close of the conference a very powerful appeal was presented to all present. Dr. Redpath asked, "Is there anybody willing to give their lives to the service of God, at home or on the mission field?" Hazel found herself in another spiritual crisis. This time she could put it off no longer. Hazel stood to her feet and in an act of full and glad surrender to the will of God she responded to the appeal.

After the Easter holidays Hazel returned to work in the shirt factory near Agnes Street where she was a supervisor. While chatting to Iris Smyth, a Christian friend in the factory, they discussed all that had happened over the holiday period. Hazel told Iris about the convention and her commitment to God. "What are you going to do now then, Hazel?" Iris inquired.

"What do you mean, what am I going to do now? I don't know what I'm going to do. What do you think I should do?" Hazel asked looking for advice.

There was silence for a second or two, then her friend went on, "I'm not very sure what you should do, but you can't stand up in a meeting like that and then just do nothing. You must do SOMETHING."

That made Hazel think. She would have to do something. And she did.

She went to see William McComb, founder and secretary of the Acre Gospel Mission. He listened to her story and, recognising the tremendous potential for God in this young woman, he recommended that she prepare for missionary service in two different ways - vocationally and spiritually. Mr. McComb recommended that Hazel should seek to train as a nurse or a teacher and then attend Bible College.

This was the counsel that Hazel had feared all along. She thought taking time to do a nursing course and then going to Bible College would take quite a few years and was somewhat daunting to someone who had never been all that keen on school or studying. Nevertheless, she accepted Mr. McComb's advice and pledged herself to God and to His work. She had already committed her "body a living sacrifice to God." Now she would have to fulfill that commitment.

In September 1953 Hazel left the shirt factory and began her nursing training at Belfast City Hospital. Over the next three years she obtained her nursing qualifications. She then proceeded to train to become a midwife. All of this training would prove to be of immense value to her in the years to come. After working for a short period in the hospital to gain experience, she then turned her attention to equipping herself spiritually for missionary work.

Hazel enrolled at The Bible College of Wales in Swansea in 1959. There she was able to spend time learning more of God's Word and developing her God-given talents through the instruction and experience of many choice servants of God.

••••

While James and Dorrie Gunning were on their second home assignment from Brazil, Hazel was accepted by Acre Gospel Mission to join the work in the distant Amazon. In July 1961, she sailed for Brazil in the company of the Gunnings.

After more than a month at sea the missionary trio finally arrived at Manaus, a city located one thousand miles upstream from the mouth of the Amazon River. The first few weeks were spent in registering Hazel's residency visa and running to and from the customs to try to release their twenty-seven pieces of baggage. During this time James took Hazel to the municipal market at the docks to introduce her to two lady missionaries who maintained a literature distribution ministry. Nell Shannon from Belfast and Dulcie Robertson from Scotland had a stall in the middle of the busy market where the locals mingled with those in transit to buy or sell their goods.

Hazel was fascinated by what she saw and was immediately attracted to this aspect of the work. She loved the hustle and bustle of the market place and the interaction the ladies had with so many people. She wanted so much to stay and help Nell and Dulcie in their work.

However, other plans awaited Hazel. Once they had cleared the baggage through customs and put the registration papers in order, Hazel travelled with James and Dorrie to Boca do Acre, a riverside town another one thousand five hundred miles farther inland from Manaus. Arriving in this interior town Hazel knew that her first priority was to give time to language study. Nouns, verbs, adjectives and strange sounding phonetics kept Hazel busy, but she could not ignore the great medical needs in the town and found that her nursing skills were in great demand.

Mollie Harvey, another missionary with Acre Gospel Mission, had already established a small clinic and a medical programme in the town of Boca do Acre. James and Dorrie's arrival allowed Mollie to return to Belfast for her scheduled and much needed furlough. Mollie was glad that Hazel, the new recruit to the work, was a nurse and midwife and therefore would be able to continue the work at the clinic.

Hazel was thrown in at the deep end. The demands and conditions were such a change from all that she had known in an established hospital back home or while on district nursing in Belfast. The new responsibilities were overwhelming. Besides all this, Hazel was continuing with her language study. An insight into the blessings and frustrations of attending the sick and needy was given by Hazel when she wrote home in 1962.

> The medical work continues to be an open door for the presentation of the gospel. During these past weeks our hearts have been saddened by the number of souls who have gone into eternity. We feel that a few of these people could have been helped with a little medical attention.
>
> On the night of Anne's (Anne McWhinnie) farewell meeting prior to going to Labrea, we were asked to go to a confinement. The old midwives requested that Dorrie and I go to a home because the case was proving to be too difficult for them. At first we were disappointed to miss the meeting for we were looking forward to giving Anne a warm sendoff. However, we sensed there was some difficulty so we went along to see the case.
>
> On our arrival, we soon discovered that they had every reason to be concerned. The poor woman had been suffering for two days, and her condition was dangerous. Four hours later she delivered a stillborn baby, which we believed had been dead for some time. We do praise God for His help in all this work. If this dear woman had been left much longer, she too would have died.
>
> In one of the little houses across the river, another woman delivered one of her twins. There was some difficulty in the second child being born. Her husband was on his way to call us when someone told him that we were already out at another case. When he got back home, he was devastated to find that his wife had already died before giving birth to the second baby.

The next day, as I was about to commence language study, there was another call. A woman who lived some distance up river was haemorrhaging. Her sister called us and said that a man would take us to her in his boat, but alas, even before we boarded the canoe, word came to say that the woman had died. The grief of this family was terrible to see. Can you understand something of our burden as we wondered just how much of the gospel that woman had ever heard? Did she or did she not hear the way of salvation?

Just a few nights ago, we were surprised when one of the men stood up in the meeting and said how the midwifery work has been a testimony for the Lord in Boca do Acre. He was referring to the first case that I mentioned in this report. The people here cannot understand how we manage to work under the difficult conditions and still remain calm. Many friends of that family have expressed their desire to attend the meetings, including the young woman who was safely delivered.

As I listened to this testimony about the medical work, the words of the hymn came to me, "Love never faileth...see, they are looking, learning of you, silently watching all that you do."

As the mission work grew the missionaries became more scattered in small towns throughout the vast Amazon region. Hazel, having already worked in the interior towns of Boca do Acre, Canutama and Sena Madureira, was asked to go to Labrea. Her work there was to assist and encourage the pastor and people in the church that had been established years earlier, rather than in the medical field

Always valuing the use of literature, Hazel purchased Bibles for use in the town and received gospel booklets from Scripture Gift Mission and the Trinitarian Bible Society. News also filtered through that the Revival Movement in Belfast, which was led by Mr. Ernie Allen, had started to print tracts in Portuguese. Soon packages of this literature began to arrive by post, and Hazel put them to very good use locally.

It was not surprising that there were many marvellous conversions during the eight years Hazel spent in Labrea. Some people trusted the Lord in the meetings, while others were awakened to their need of Christ without even meeting a missionary.

Perhaps no conversion was more dramatic than that of a man called Raimundo Lobato. As a young man of eighteen, Raimundo lived in a distant and remote part of the forest. He and those who lived in that region made their meagre living from gathering Brazil nuts and extracting rubber latex from the syringa trees. They hunted and fished for their daily provisions.

Raimundo and a friend would often go on hunting expeditions to look for wild boar or deer. Once they hunted down the wild animal, they would salt the meat and bring it back to the settlement to share with their families and neighbours. On one such expedition, after the two young men had been hunting for three days, Raimundo's companion became ill and burned with a roaring fever. Raimundo helped him into his hammock, which he had suspended between two trees, since he was too ill to trek back to their settlement. Raimundo despaired when the young man sank into unconsciousness. In spite of all that Raimundo tried to do for him, his friend died a short time later. There was no way Raimundo could carry the corpse back to the settlement, a two-day trek away. He had no other option than to wrap his friend's body in a hammock and bury him in a shallow grave.

When Raimundo arrived back without his friend, the people were stunned to hear the news of the young man's death, but no one was more dazed than Raimundo Lobato. The sudden death of his companion prompted him to ask probing questions about death, eternity, heaven and hell. When he spoke to his uncle about the matter, he said that he had an old Bible that he had picked up at one time. He gave the tattered volume to his nephew who began to slowly read the scriptures. Someone told Raimundo to tune his radio to the short-wave and listen to Trans World Radio. Through the influence of the printed page and the radio, without ever having met a missionary or another Christian, Raimundo trusted the Saviour and called upon God for mercy in the heart of the Brazilian forest.

After his conversion Raimundo read the scriptures each night to the others in the settlement during the customary hour of the Catholic Novena. Within a few months almost forty people in that jungle clearing were converted without contact from outside missionary influences.

The more Raimundo read the scriptures, the more he wanted to know about Christ and to follow Him. Eager to be baptized, he decided to go to Labrea or Canutama, the nearest towns. Travel by boat to either of these towns took almost three weeks, so Raimundo decided to walk through the jungle – in that way he could make it in ten days. He trekked to Labrea and arrived at the mission house where he requested to be baptized by the pastor. It was a memorable day for Raimundo as he shared his amazing testimony with the people gathered at the side of the River Purus and then was baptized by Pastor Jose Salsa.

Having tasted of the fellowship with the believers at the church in Labrea, Raimundo decided he would go back to the forest, gather his belongings and return to town so he could enjoy God's people. Providentially, Hazel was working with the church in Labrea at this time, and she took this new convert under her wing and encouraged him in his Christian life. Raimundo was keen to learn. His reading skills were more guess work than actually discerning the letters, so Hazel painstakingly helped him sharpen up. The church gave him opportunity to develop his preaching ability, and it soon became evident that this young man had good potential for Christian work

Raimundo Lobato was not satisfied to remain in Labrea. Hazel received news of a new Baptist Bible Institute in Manaus, the capital of Amazonas, specifically set up to train young men from the interior. Within a year, Raimundo left Labrea to enroll at this Bible Institute and was greatly supported by Hazel in this step. While at Bible college, Raimundo met and married Cila who came from another distant part of Amazonas. After graduation, the young newly weds returned to Labrea where Raimundo became the pastor of his home church. Later he received a call to the Canutama church, and after a short spell there, he and his family returned to Manaus where he has pastored several churches. All that the result of reading literature in the heart of the jungle, in a place the missionaries had not yet reached. This had a significant influence on Hazel's future ministry

••••

Change lay ahead for Hazel but she was not aware of it at first. Sometimes changes are the result of conscious decisions we make, while other changes are uninvited and thrust upon us. However, they are no less part of God's plan for us to accomplish His purpose.

Throughout the years that Hazel worked in these interior towns she maintained contact with Nell Shannon and Dulcie Robertson, the veteran independent missionaries she met when she first arrived in Manaus in 1961. After more than thirty years' work at the market, Nell had to return to Northern Ireland while Dulcie continued with the witness at the bookstall.

These two ladies were always good friends with the Acre missionaries, and when Nell retired to Northern Ireland and Dulcie to London they donated their house to Acre Gospel Mission. One day in 1983 Victor Maxwell received a call from Dulcie to inform him that she too had to return to the United Kingdom urgently. She explained that due to her sudden departure she was anxious for someone to take her place at the market and asked Victor if anyone from the Acre Mission would be available to take it over.

At that time, Hazel was still working in Labrea but was becoming increasingly conscious that her work there was finished. She was keen for a new challenge in her ministry but was not sure where that might be. Dulcie's appeal corresponded with a visit Victor and Audrey Maxwell planned to make to Canutama and Labrea to open a new church. While in Labrea they shared the news of Nell and Dulcie's retirement with Hazel and put to her the challenge of their literature ministry at the market. It was immediately obvious to Hazel this was God's next step for her and His timing was perfect. Right away Hazel responded positively to the invitation and within a few days was on her way to Manaus.

When Hazel arrived in Manaus Dulcie Robertson had already left for England, so there was no one available to orientate Hazel in how to go about this work. First of all, she realized she had to establish her place at the market as others were keen to usurp the place that Dulcie had left. The market was a noted centre for spiritist and voodoo shops, so after much prayer and claiming the protection of the mighty name of the Lord Jesus, Hazel arrived at the market on the first day at 7.00 a.m. She claimed her spot and stood her ground in spite of some traders and other antagonists trying to put pressure on her to leave.

Hazel then had to ensure a continuous supply of literature. Urgent letters were dispatched to various publishing houses, including Every Home Crusade in Belfast, appealing to them to send gospel tracts and booklets. Within weeks plentiful supplies of gospel literature arrived. Hazel was at her market place early each morning. Her work near the gateway of the market made an immediate impact on many passersby.

Allen Loney wrote of that work some years later:

Hazel arrived in Manaus just when Miss Dulcie Robertson was ready to hand over the ministry at the market, where she and Nell Shannon had faithfully stood with their display of gospel literature for many years.

Every morning Monday through Saturday at seven o'clock, Hazel leaves the Mission house carrying her bags of books and leaflets. She walks down the crowded streets to the big market in the centre of the city and near the waterfront in Manaus. The rough pavements are thronged with people going about their business. Hazel is conscious that she is about her Father's business.

As she approaches the market, the thoroughfare narrows. People file past hordes of street vendors who have taken over most of the footpath with their stalls, which are cluttered with all sorts of goods. Little children and their mothers try to sell shopping bags, fruit, or vegetables in the doorways.

Eventually, Hazel reaches the huge enclosed market with its grey walls and three lovely wrought iron gateways. She heads through the central gate and just inside, she unlocks a wooden chest that quickly unfolds into a Bible and tract display. A poster, *The Broad and Narrow Way*, is displayed on an adjacent pillar. Another poster announces *The Two Calls*, which depicts a rich man sitting at his desk, too busy to attend to the evangelist. At the bottom of the poster are startling words, "Thou fool, this night thy soul shall be required of thee."

Hazel has tracts in her hands and starts to distribute them to all who enter through the gates. Although ignored by many and scoffed at by some, she does have opportunity to speak to many others. Once Hazel gains their attention, soon she is able to show them the way of salvation through Jesus Christ. Through this daily witness, Hazel led hundreds of people to Jesus Christ. Many of the converts return to ask advice from Hazel or request literature to use in their witness for Jesus Christ.

Perhaps the most remarkable conversion at the gateway was that of Manuel, one of the local traders who was raised in a spiritist family but was hungry for the truth of the gospel. He was struck by Hazel's zealous approach to evangelism near to where he was trying to make a living. This enthusiasm and sincerity soon got to him, and after reading the literature, he not only accepted Jesus Christ as his Saviour but also became one of her greatest supporters at the market.

When another young man named Marcos accepted the Saviour at the gateway, he wept. Like Manuel, he also came from a spiritist background but after his conversion, he went home and told his family about the Saviour. His mother, father and then his brothers and sisters came to the Saviour.

Beyond the work at the market Hazel was challenged by the need and opportunity in the city plazas where hundreds of students congregated each night. All high schools in Manaus operate for all ages in the evenings in order to accommodate thousands of teenagers who cannot attend school during the day. Hazel saw this as a great mission field and opportunity to put the Word of God into the hands of these students. She solicited the help of some young men to help her distribute the scriptures to these masses.

Armed with Every Home Crusade literature Hazel visited the campuses of different schools several evenings each week to make contact with these young people. She recruited many young people from local churches to help in this evangelistic outreach. Through this endeavour many students came to the Saviour. Hercules was a down-and-out drug addict whom Hazel met on the street and led to Jesus Christ. She then helped sponsor him at a rehabilitation clinic. Today, he is the resident caretaker of a church in Manaus.

Several of the young people who accompanied Hazel in her outreach work were later called into full-time Christian ministry. Hazel put some of the young Bible college students to work at the market and would use that as a way to support them during their training. One such young man was Elias. Hazel taught Elias English and supported him during his studies at the Baptist Seminary of Amazonas. Elias was burdened and enthusiastic about the ministry at the market and substituted for Hazel on the occasion when she had to travel to the United Kingdom. He also engaged in evangelism to the multitudes of passengers from the many boats that were docked nearby. Today Elias has a degree in theology, speaks four languages, and pastors a church in North East Brazil.

The effect of drugs and alcohol on so many young people prompted Hazel to request that Ernie Allen and the staff of Every Home Crusade would supply her with a broadsheet that would highlight the dangers of abuse from drink and drugs. Mr. Allen was glad to be able to supply tea chests full of illustrated broadsheets which portrayed *The Horrors of Booze* in cartoons and booklets teaching *The Way of Salvation*.

Day after day at the gateway of the central market Hazel distributed these broadsheets and leaflets. She took time to have a personal word with many who stopped to speak with her. During the years in which Hazel carried on this ministry she was able to lead hundreds of anxious people to personal faith in Jesus Christ. She also supplied many pastors and evangelists with Every Home Crusade literature, and reports came back of much blessing through this distribution.

The years of literature witness were not without mishaps and setbacks. One Wednesday Hazel arrived home at noon from the market. She was brimming with enthusiasm that she had met a man who was a representative for a Christian Publishing House in the south of Brazil and was selling Bibles at wholesale prices. She told Victor that the man would be calling at the Mission house shortly with some of these Bibles, so she needed her dollars from the safe.

As good as his word, the well-dressed young man arrived at the Mission house and was very courteous in showing the range of Bibles he carried - zipped Bibles, small Bibles, large Bibles. He told Hazel he was prepared to sell them at a fifty per cent discount of the retail price. Without any hesitation, Hazel told Victor to take all the Bibles.

The total bill came to just under $500.00. The young man provided a receipt, and then Hazel placed an order for another quantity of Bibles for when the young man would return to Manaus. No deposit was needed for this order. After the salesman left, there was general thanksgiving for this providential contact.

On the following Saturday, not long after lunch, several of the missionaries were taking their afternoon siesta when they were disturbed by someone knocking at the front door. Missionary colleague, Emily Gilchrist, attended the door, only to be confronted by three men. They asked if this was the Mission house, to which Emily replied positively. Although they were in plain clothes, they announced that they were policemen.

Emily became a little nervous at this news, for she had been to the Bank of Brasil a few days previously when the manager impounded her $100 bill which she had purchased from the Ulster Bank in Belfast. The bank manager informed her the note was a counterfeit. He refused to give her the exchange or to return the hundred dollar bill. Besides losing the money, which Emily believed to be perfectly legitimate, she now thought these policemen had come to arrest her.

One of the officers sensed that Emily was somewhat taken aback and immediately disclosed the purpose of his visit. He said he had come to inquire about the theft of Bibles. Emily was somewhat relieved that at least the police had not come to arrest her.

Emily called for Hazel. Instead of having a siesta, Hazel was in the basement of the house preparing a recorded message to send to her friends in Bangor, telling them about the great bargain of new Bibles. When she heard that the police were at the door, she came to the door immediately and wanted to know where Victor was. Emily said Victor and Audrey had gone to meet their daughters, who were coming home from the missionary boarding school for the weekend.

Hazel politely confronted the three men by asking, "How do I know you are policemen?"

The leader produced his wallet and showed his police identity badge. He then produced the copy of the order Hazel had given to the young man on Mission paper and said, "That young man was a thief. He bought those Bibles at the Evangelical bookstore with a cheque that bounced. I know that you have nothing to do with the crime, but if you still have the Bibles we will take them back to the owner and nothing more will be said about the matter to you."

Hazel had only sold a few of the Bibles, and the majority of them were still in boxes in her apartment. She lost no time in bringing them out of storage and handing them over to the man, with a mixture of disappointment and relief.

As the three men carried the boxes out to a waiting car, Hazel followed them and spied the original salesman sitting in the rear seat of a Chevette with a gun pointed into his side by another plain clothes officer. The young man seemed to be in distress and was crying. He shouted to Hazel that he was sorry.

Hazel waved her arm and retreated with haste before closing the door.

"Where is Victor?" Hazel called. "Wait 'til he hears what happened."

About a week later, after all had settled down, Victor met David Van Beveran, the missionary in charge of the Evangelical bookstore and related the story to him. David affirmed that Bibles had been bought against a check that bounced and was glad to hear that the police had caught the thief. In turn he went to the police station to find out what had happened to the stolen merchandise. On hearing the details, the police officers told him that the missionaries must have been conned twice. The thief and the so called "policemen" were all part of the same gang who had probably sold, recovered and resold the Bibles several times.

Notwithstanding these setbacks, Hazel continued to maintain the witness at the market for the next fourteen years, until her mother's deteriorating health forced her to retire from Brazil. In her absence Brazilian missionaries still continue the strategic literature ministry at the gateway to the market in Manaus. Every Home Crusade still provides the tools to fulfill this ministry by furnishing the missionaries with a supply of booklets, tracts and gospels.

# 7

# BACK IN AFRICA WITH THE GOSPEL
## *Alan and Dorothy Graham*

The loose canvas flaps fluttered in the gentle breeze which rippled across the old gospel tent. The 'canvas cathedral' had been pitched on a green in the heart of Rathcoole Estate, just outside Belfast, for a two-week gospel crusade.

Alan Graham emerged from his granny's house across the road from the tent and couldn't help noticing the bold capital letters, which spelt out the simple message, "GOD LOVES YOU." It was the message Alan Graham needed to hear for he was despairing of his life and future.

Underneath the sign, at the open door of the tent, stood Alan's younger and only brother Joe, a Christian and one of the workers from BethShan Gospel Tabernacle on Belfast's Shankill Road. Joe was one of the outreach workers involved in the special evangelistic crusade.

In his heart Alan wished that he could be like Joe, but he wasn't. Whereas Joe had become a Christian, Alan wasn't. He felt his life was in a mess, his marriage seemed to be on the slippery slopes and heading for the divorce courts. *How could I ever change Dorothy?* Alan wondered. *How could my life ever change? What if I lose the children?* The thoughts troubled him.

Just then another Christian offered Alan and the family a ride into the city. Alan gladly accepted the offer for his financial circumstances were not great. Furthermore, Alan calculated that an extra few pennies would pay for another bottle of beer.

Joe was aware that all was not well between Alan and Dorothy. He was not only concerned for his brother and sister-in-law, but also for their two children, Mandy and Gary. He quietly prayed for them.

Alan was the eldest of Mr. & Mrs. Graham's three children, with Joe being two years younger than Alan and Karen another three years younger than Joe. The three children had been reared on the Shankill Road in the days before the 'troubles' began in Belfast in 1969. Alan attended the Church of God Sunday School in Percy Street on the lower Shankill with his brother and sister and learned the Bible lessons from their keen teachers.

Alan's attendance at Riddle Memorial Primary School and Somerdale Secondary School was not particularly outstanding other than his developing a keen interest in all kinds of sporting activities providing they kept him out of the classroom. Alan had more interest in a ball than in books. He became a devotee to football, basketball and cricket and was quite competent at all of these.

He not only became engrossed in sport; he developed enough soccer skills to gain a place on the school football team and from there went on to play in various teams in different soccer leagues in Northern Ireland.

When he was fourteen years old Alan left Sunday School, but not before giving a lot of thought to becoming a Christian. Sunday School teachers had impressed upon his young mind his individual need of salvation. Alan knew that he was a sinner who needed to be saved and that Jesus Christ was the only Saviour. However, although he was almost persuaded to become a Christian, yet he resisted taking that important step because of peer pressure. He was afraid of what people might say.

Resistance to the gospel does not leave the sinner in a vacuum. Alan not only succumbed to peer pressure, but the very same companions that took him from the things of God, also enticed him to a fascination for alcoholic beverages. That fascination soon became an alcoholic addiction. Even though he spent time in physical training to prepare for football games, yet he was nullifying any advantage by imbibing vast amounts of liquor.

Like many other young men from the area, after finishing his education at Somerdale Secondary School, Alan secured a job as an apprentice fitter at Mackies Engineering Works. By this time the Belfast troubles had escalated to a severe pitch with random bombings, numerous murders and political agitation on the streets.

Early in 1972 Alan received an invitation from an uncle and aunt to go and join them for a new life in Rhodesia. He decided to take up the offer. Later that year, 3 weeks before leaving for Rhodesia, he went to Liverpool to go and see the famous Liverpool 'Reds' play their local rivals Everton at Anfield Stadium. He enjoyed the local derby game and to celebrate Liverpool's one-goal victory over Everton Alan could not resist a drinking binge, which is all too common after many soccer matches. The celebration was so good Alan missed the return sailing to Belfast.

Missing the Belfast boat made a lasting impression on Alan's life and did him a good turn. Had he been on the sailing that night he might never have met Dorothy Beamish, a seventeen-year-old Scouser who came in pursuit of a friend who was to be at the same bar where Alan was drinking. For Alan it was more than love at first sight. Even before he spoke to the young woman he knew he had fallen in love with her instantly. Soon he engineered a way to chat her up and this only confirmed the initial feeling he felt for this Liverpool lass. After the first encounter Alan and Dorothy began to date. Alan was so madly in love with Dorothy that he wanted to marry her immediately but her Dad would not give consent because she was too young.

Instead of going to Rhodesia Alan decided to take a job in Liverpool so that he could be near to Dorothy to whom he became engaged just three months later. As per her father's instructions, Dorothy waited until she was eighteen years old before walking down the aisle to tie the knot with Alan. She was eighteen on Wednesday 22nd August 1973 and Alan and Dorothy were married on 25th August 1973.

One year after they were married the newlyweds reverted to Alan's original plan and headed off for a new life in Rhodesia. Even though this southern African country was being convulsed by the transition of independence and nationhood, life was great as the young couple set up home in Bulawayo. The weather seemed to be perfect for outdoor living, there were plenty of opportunities for sports and the booze was plentiful and cheap.

For the next four years Alan and Dorothy enjoyed a merry life style. Alan found employment at the Rhodesian Railways before moving to the Steel works at Redcliffe. The birth of their little daughter, Mandy Claire, on 24th April 1976, only added to their happiness.

That perceived happiness was greatly flawed when excessive drinking began to take its toll and Alan and Dorothy's lives began to creep apart. Alan later admitted that his immoderate drinking binges made him extremely selfish and made his wife and baby daughter suffer. They tried to make their marriage work and hold together, but it was difficult.

During her second pregnancy the family made a visit back to Ireland. During the six-week holiday Alan met up with his old friends and visited the former drinking haunts. He went through £3500.00 on alcohol during that period. While they were back in Belfast they decided to go back to Rhodesia, pack up their belongings and return to Northern Ireland. However, they came home to nothing; no money, no home and no job.

They were able to stay at Alan's Mum and Dad's home while Alan went job hunting. Soon he was able to go back to his job as a fitter at Mackies and later found alternative employment at Short's Aircraft factory. With some income they were able to put a deposit on a house and move in. Gary Alan, their second child was born on 8th June 1978.

Although they were all under one roof the marriage relationship continued to deteriorate. The aunt, with whom they had gone to live in Rhodesia, returned home to Ulster. Alan and the children went to visit with her at his grandmother's house in Rathcoole. While there Alan slipped out of the house to go to a nearby shop to buy cigarettes. It was then he was confronted with the view of the gospel tent and the pertinent message, "GOD LOVES YOU."

After Alan arrived home with the children Dorothy went out with Joe and his wife Rachel. Unknown to Alan Joe had invited Dorothy to attend the meeting in the tent at Rathcoole. Alan remained at home and downed six cans of Harp, his favourite beer.

It was only when she returned home that Alan learned she had been to the meeting. "Did you get saved?" Alan asked.

"What would you know about getting saved?" Dorothy retorted in a rage. Although she had been sent to Sunday School as a child Dorothy had no real influence of the gospel in her life.

As Alan relates of those days, "It was all picture and no sound. There wasn't much love in the home and when we did speak it was only to shout at and devour each other."

From his Sunday School days Alan still understood the simple steps of the gospel and his personal need of salvation through Christ. "If you get saved I'll change," he persisted to Dorothy."

"You saved?" Dorothy replied with venom. "No. You're finished. It's all over with us."

That night sleep did not come easily. Alan lay awake thinking about and deeply regretting his empty and wasted life. He remembered the days at Sunday School and what the Lord Jesus had done for him at Calvary. He felt determined to do something about the plight of his marriage and the mess he had got himself into.

On the following morning Dorothy agreed to go to the tent with him that Monday evening. Baby sitters were arranged and the struggling couple went to the meeting. Little can be remembered of what the preacher spoke on but Alan was deeply concerned for his spiritual welfare.

This concern constrained Alan to return to the tent on Tuesday night. He listened intently to the preacher and tears flowed freely at the conclusion of the meeting. Joe invited Alan to speak with the preacher rather than go home in that state. Alan declined the invitation.

At home Alan could not silence the voice that was speaking to his inner man. He went to bed, tossed and turned, first one way and then another, but sleep would not come. Finally, in desperation, Alan got out of bed and on his knees called on God for mercy and salvation. He asked the Lord Jesus to come into his heart and life. Peace and assurance flooded his heart and after some time he returned to bed.

On the next morning he said nothing to Dorothy about what had happened during the night. At Shorts he told some work mates he had become a Christian. Most of them laughed at him but Alan knew his life was changed and he was not for returning to the old life. Later that morning George McKimm, now a pastor in Scotland, invited Alan to attend a lunch hour Bible Study at the factory.

For the first time in his life Alan felt the warmth of Christian fellowship as other believers welcomed him to the study. He was so happy going home that night. He tried to hug Dorothy at home and tell her what had happened the previous night. She would not believe it and thought Alan was up to some trick again.

It took twenty-four hours for Dorothy to accept that Alan really had changed. The old ways and attitudes had evidently gone. Dorothy could only conclude that her husband had been born again. That night Alan took Dorothy to Rathcoole again and at the end of the meeting she received the Lord Jesus Christ as Saviour.

Everything was new for Mr. and Mrs. Graham. Their marriage had been rescued and the children noticed the difference. Their parents could not deny the transformation. Dorothy was astounded when Alan handed over his unopened pay packet. Previously he deducted his drinking money before giving Dorothy the balance to run the house for the week. Salvation had brought a bonus and Dorothy's household money was almost doubled. "Those drinking days are gone

Dorothy. This is our money. Now we need to think of giving our offerings to the Lord."

When brother Joe came to see the happy couple he encouraged them greatly. He explained to them the principle of tithing their income and honouring the Lord with their substance. There were many financial demands to maintain their growing children but the newly converted couple endeavoured to honour God.

At church, BethShan Tabernacle, they felt their minds were blown away. God's presence was so real. The Bible was a new book. When Saturday came Alan paced the floor and wondered what he should do instead of going to his favourite drinking place, the Deer's Head Bar in Lower Garfield Street. He finally decided he would go back to his old drinking haunt. Dorothy pleaded with him not to go. She was even more concerned when he explained that this time he was going on a mission. He planned to go to the Deer's Head armed with a good supply of gospel tracts to witness for the Lord.

Alan prayed the Lord would help him before arriving at the bar. As was normal, Alan's dad, who was also his best friend, was there for his regular round of drink. He nearly died with embarrassment when he saw Alan with a bunch of tracts in his hand telling former drinking friends about his conversion. Someone called out, "Give Grahamer a pint and a half'n."

Alan confidently answered, "Grahamer doesn't need that anymore. Grahamer's saved."

As he left the bar a weight seemed to fall off Alan's shoulders. He was ecstatic and joy filled his heart. He felt he had obeyed the Lord. The alcohol days were gone. Alan's father, poor man, said it was the worst day he had ever spent in a pub.

It wasn't long before Alan and Dorothy were totally involved in the work at BethShan. Besides attending the regular meetings, Alan was there for the door to door visitation, the Youth club, the Sunday School.

Henry Berry of Child Evangelism Fellowship paid a visit to the Tabernacle and challenged all present about reaching boys and girls for the Saviour. As Henry spoke of Good News Clubs, Five-Day

Clubs and various opportunities for children's ministry Alan was aware of God speaking to him, "This is the work I have for you." He knew it was God's call.

On the following Monday evening Alan went to the Children's meeting at his church. The two ladies who tried to control the forty children and conduct the meeting were glad to see some muscle. Until then Alan had thought that grace was something a Christian said before a meal but that night he needed the grace of God to restrain him. Several of the boys were little toughs who tried to create mayhem. Alan grabbed them by the scruff the neck and forcibly made them sit down and be quiet.

The two ladies were so impressed by the attention and respect Alan commanded in the meeting that night. The children listened like they had never done before. At the end of the meeting the two ladies nominated Alan and elected him to take control of the Children's Meeting. He had little say in the matter.

Alan was dumbfounded with the new responsibility. In the emergency he phoned Henry Berry who introduced Alan to his first CEF Teacher Training Seminar in BethShan Tabernacle. After that Alan and Dorothy were invited to the Annual CEF Weekend at Portrush and then to various CEF conferences at Kilkeel and other locations. Both of them were overwhelmed when Joe Kennedy spoke of the opportunities and challenges of leading camps in the Republic of Ireland.

Alan was a volunteer worker at a CEF camp at Dunkineely in Donegal the next summer. He loved the involvement with the thirty children from Sligo and Donegal so much. His experience at camp only deepened the conviction that children's ministry was their niche and couldn't wait to return to Dunkineely the following summer.

Joe Kennedy, the CEF worker in Sligo, was so impressed by Alan's enthusiasm and competence with children he asked Alan what they were doing in Belfast. Alan shared that they were involved in the children's work of their local church and whatever opportunities might arise. Joe then challenged Alan to consider giving it all up and go to work with boys and girls in the much neglected West of Ireland.

Alan shared Joe's challenge with Dorothy when he arrived home and they decided to pray about the matter. "God if you want us to go to Dunkineely, Delhi, Donaghadee, or Donegal, we are willing to go. Please show to us Your will."

God answered that prayer at the next CEF Easter conference at Portrush when Tom Bathgate spoke from the words of Jesus in John 4:35, "Say not ye, There are yet four months, and then cometh harvest? Behold, I say unto you, Lift up your eyes, and look on the fields; for they are white already to harvest." Both Alan and Dorothy knew it was time to take the first steps to full-time ministry with boys and girls.

Alan arranged an appointment with David McQuilken, the Director of CEF in Ireland. David advised that Alan should study for at least a year at Bible College. To go to Bible College was a major step for the Graham family. The tuition for the year at the Assemblies of God Bible College in Mattersey, England, was £2,200.00 and they had £96.00 in savings. Furthermore, Dorothy would have to stay at home and care for the children without a regular wage coming in. Although they wondered how they could manage it all, they decided to step out in faith. Alan applied for a place at the college for September 1984.

Just two days after they application was sent Alan and Dorothy discovered that God had already taken care of the college fees. Although they hadn't told anyone that Alan had made application to the college two friends came to see him. They told Alan and Dorothy that for more than a year they had a witness that Alan would go to Bible College and in anticipation of that step they had been saving money. They placed in Alan's hands enough to pay the full tuition fee for the whole year.

In those early steps of faith Alan and Dorothy learned the truth of the maxim coined many years earlier by Hudson Taylor, "God's work, done in God's way, will not lack God's supply." In trusting God to supply their needs they determined not to apply for supplementary benefit from the government. Dorothy decided to look for a job to keep her busy while Alan was away and to help their finances at home.

Just when Alan left for England a milkman came to the door and left two pints of milk. Dorothy was sure he had made a mistake and was afraid to use the milk. On the next day the milkman met her and asked if she had discovered the milk he left at her door. She confessed she did but did not know what to do with it. "I'll be God's milkman for you and deliver milk every day while Alan's away."

A few days later a coal truck drew up at the door. "Can you take a few bags of coal?" asked the coalman whose cheerful face was masked and smeared with coal dust. Dorothy affirmed that she could. "I'll be God's coalman to you while Alan is away," said the Christian friend after he delivered two bags into the coalbunker.

On Friday the butcher called Dorothy and told her to go down to his shop as he had something for her. When she got there he gave her a bag with an assortment of meats, enough to do the family all week. "Come back next Friday and I will have another bag for you. I'll be your butcher while Alan is away," he assured Dorothy who was overwhelmed by so much kindness.

God did not provide what they needed by sending ravens with meat as in the days of Elijah, but His faithfulness and provision was just as timely and precise as in the days of the prophets. Dorothy was able to secure a job as a home-help to three different homes nearby. This allowed her to be at home when the children needed their mother and also gave her a monthly wage of £91.00. The mortgage cost £90.00 each month. Family and friends rallied round the Graham family and during that year they lacked for nothing.

Meanwhile, Alan was able to pick up the theological studies at college and gain the utmost benefit from the lectures and studies during that year. Three months after finishing at college Alan went on to Kilchzimmer in Switzerland to complete the CEF specialised training course before making application to the Mission. Again he was challenged by the need all over Europe. With each challenge he surrendered to God for wherever the Lord would want to use Him, but through all this, Alan still felt that Donegal was the place God had laid on his heart and he would not be derailed.

They applied and were accepted by CEF and after a short period of working with Eric Friel in the North and West Belfast area, they went to Donegal in 1987. In a miraculous way God provided a super home for them but they were anxious to get started in the real work they had gone to do, reaching boys and girls for Jesus Christ.

Initially they tried to gain entrance into the schools. The teachers and principals said they would be glad to have Alan and Dorothy visit the schools and conduct classes. However, a particular influential priest barred the way. Not to be outdone, Alan went to see the Bishop. He shared his testimony in a most diplomatic way and told what God had done in his life. The Bishop was so impressed that he opened the door for Alan to have access into a hundred and six Catholic schools in his diocese.

Alan was not slow to seize the opportunity and in some of those schools he conducted Bible teaching classes for a week before the principal sensed that what Alan taught was contrary to what the Mother Church taught. In other schools he was able to carry on with the gospel outreach for more than three years before they were asked to leave because of pressure from the Mother church. During the intervening time Alan and Dorothy were able to reach thousands and thousands of children with the gospel.

The parents of a child in one such school took Alan to court in an attempt to have him expelled because of the 'heresy' he was teaching their child. In spite of the pressure, the headmaster who loved the Saviour, refused to bow to the demands. When several families and the clergy tried to gang up on the headmaster he refused to budge. He was a man of principle and rather than give in to the bigotry and discrimination, he finally resigned his post and returned to farming.

Running parallel with the involvement with the schools Alan and Dorothy conducted a very effective camp ministry during the summer. Up to four hundred boys and girls attended the camp each year, first at Lissadell in Sligo and then to the new camp centre in Rossnowlagh, Donegal.

During those years in Donegal hundreds of these children came to know Jesus Christ as personal Saviour. Many of them are still going on with God and finding His direction for their lives. The camps continue and some of the children, who were converted during Alan's ministry in the West of Ireland, are leaders at the camps today.

In 1996 Alan had opportunity to go to Romania when CEF colleague, the late Tom Somerville, invited Alan to speak at their field leadership conference up in the mountains. Alan's theme for the week was, "The Fruit of the Spirit" and he had a wonderful time ministering the Word of God. The conference made a big change in Alan and Dorothy's lives. During that week Alan had time to wait in God's presence as he took unhurried time to read through the book of Acts. During those hours God impressed upon Alan that the Lord had something more for him.

During the next few weeks Alan travelled over Romania preaching the Word of God but he could not get away from this inner conviction that God had something else for Him to do. In a gentle way God brought Alan to another crisis in his life. He sensed that God was speaking, "Alan, you are in a comfort zone. If you would yield all of your life to Me I will do so much more through you." Alan bowed in worshipful submission to the Saviour and again surrendered to whatever the Lord Jesus had for him.

On returning to Donegal Alan shared with Dorothy how God had spoken to him. Dorothy's immediate reaction was, "Alan, I'm not going to Romania. We left Northern Ireland to come here to Donegal and there is no way I am for leaving here." Dorothy even refused to pray about the matter for the next eight months.

Coming near to Christmas Alan reminded Dorothy of the day they prayed and said, "Lord, Donaghadee, Donegal, Delhi or wherever, we are willing to go anywhere for Jesus." Alan probed a little more and asked, "Dorothy, did we really mean that prayer or were they just empty words?"

Dorothy broke down in tears and realised she had strayed from the place of willingness and submission to the Saviour. Both of them got on their knees and repented before the Lord. As best they knew how, they yielded themselves to whatever He might have for them.

Early in 1998 they attended a meeting in Londonderry where a friend was preaching. In the course of his address the friend said, "There is a promised land lying ahead but you won't get into that promised land unless you have your feet in the water."

His friend's words impressed Alan so much that he wrote in his notebook, "What is my promised land?" As the preacher continued the Lord seemed to be impressing Africa on Alan's heart. He shared this with Dorothy afterwards and she asked, "Africa? Why Africa?"

"I don't know." answered Alan, "We did spend four years there in our unregenerate days. Maybe that has something to do with it. Let us just pray about it and see what the Lord shows us." Pray about they did.

Just coming up to their twenty-fifth wedding anniversary Alan suggested they make a Joshua-and-Caleb trip to Zimbabwe (formerly Rhodesia) and spy out the land. They arrived in Harare, capital of Zimbabwe, without knowing anybody in the city. However, they did feel very drawn to the place and believed that God was leading them to this city. Twenty years earlier they had lived in Zimbabwe's second city, Bulawayo, a much smaller town. At that time they hated Harare which had now grown to more than three million of a population. In spite of their former dislike for the city they fell in love with it during this visit and felt constrained that this is where God wanted them to start a work for CEF.

On returning to Donegal they continued to seek God to know His will and asked God to show them the way. At Easter they made their way to Portrush for the Annual CEF Convention where Pastor David McFarland was preaching. Alan and Dorothy had prayed that if the Lord was in their thoughts about Zimbabwe then let one of the speakers mention Africa during the weekend. They made this request to the Lord knowing it was most unlikely that anyone should mention the dark continent as CEF Ireland comes under the umbrella of European CEF and the emphasis would probably be placed there.

During the conference Pastor McFarland touched and challenged their lives when he said that often in the ministry it is easy to settle into a comfort zone of service, just going round in circles without accomplishing much for God. The preacher said, "It is time to step out for God."

At the end of the conference Alan and Dorothy clearly heard God speak when Pastor McFarland asked the CEF Director for Ireland, Mr. Berry, "For thirty years CEF has been sending missionaries to Europe. Why is it they have never sent anyone to Africa?"

Just as Isaiah of old heard God ask, "Also I heard the voice of the Lord, saying, 'Whom shall I send, and who will go for us?'" Alan and Dorothy knew it was the Lord's voice and in their hearts they answered, "Here are we; send us."

When they went to speak to Henry Berry about what God had put in their hearts he was already anticipating their approach and said to them, "Alan and Dorothy, I know what you have come to see me about. You feel God is opening the door to go to Africa. Go for it and the Lord be with you."

Back in Donegal they shared with Mandy and Gary what God had put in their hearts and how God had spoken to them at the conference. Both Mandy and Gary were studying at Queen's University in Belfast at this time. When they heard of the possibility of the family moving to Zimbabwe there were many tears. The whole family loved Donegal. They were emotionally attached to many friends, not to mention the ministry to so many boys and girls. However, Mandy and Gary would not stand in the way of their parents. They laid their hands on their parents as they prayed and released them to pursue what God had put in their hearts.

Just as it was not easy to leave Donegal, it was even more difficult to obtain a visa for Zimbabwe. In the African nation there was a lot of agitation and unrest. Because of this there was great resistance to Europeans entering the country and most certainly a white missionary was not particularly welcome. As a matter of fact, the general trend was for the whites to be leaving the country.

In spite of all the difficulties, the Lord opened the door for Alan and Dorothy when they obtained a three-year permit to reside in Zimbabwe. They fell in love with the country all over again. Although they knew no one in the city they quickly found their feet and got themselves established. A quick survey indicated to them the great need in the rural bush areas. Very soon they embarked on the CEF ministry to boys and girls in the more remote and isolated regions.

Once they got their Good-News-Club programme under way they were reaching up to ten thousand children every week in these remote regions. Opportunities abounded to conduct seminars and Good News Clubs in schools. In some cases Alan and Dorothy witnessed to whole schools, the teachers as well as the children, repenting and receiving Jesus Christ as Saviour. While serving in these rural areas Alan was able to distribute Gospel of John booklets which had been sent by Every Home Crusade, to thousands of children. They not only treasured these booklets, but Alan has been told that a single gospel booklet is read at least ten times.

Alan wrote to Every Home Crusade about this special outreach ministry;

> Yesterday we taught in Cresta Breeders School and after the lesson on Zaccheus I gave an invitation to receive the Lord Jesus and two hundred responded. WOW! We need much wisdom in following up these very poor children as many come from abusive homes filled with alcohol and witchcraft. Pray for us and please pray for them. An interesting thing happened as we left the school. One of the children wanted to shake my hand and then everyone did the same. That is more than four hundred handshakes. When I asked the head master why they wanted to shake hands he explained that I was the first white man (marungo) who ever touched them or had shown any interest in them.

Another letter to Every Home Crusade spoke of the worsening political situation in Zimbabwe, which endangered the safety of the CEF team;

> The situation here in Zimbabwe seems to be deteriorating daily with violence, fuel shortages and 70% inflation. The cost of foodstuffs is unreal, most things are more expensive now than what they would be in UK and Ireland BUT our hope and trust is in our God. We were at an all night prayer meeting last week with three thousand other believers. It was awesome. God came amongst us in a mighty way and drove all fear away. Please pray about the whole situation. Many whites are leaving but we believe God has called us here and He will keep us. Amen!

Alan kept in regular contact with Every Home Crusade, not only appreciating their work to produce the gospel literature that he and the team were using, but also for their prayer fellowship. He wrote of this in the following letter,

> We thank you for your love and prayers for us this past week as we ventured forth with the gospel in to the Mashonaland, the West district of Zimbabwe.
> Truly the Lord was with us and we give Him all the glory for what was achieved in His name. We left Harare on Sunday 14th May and stayed on our friend's farm in Raffingora. His house was invaded by "war veterans" a few weeks ago and we were not sure about going on this trip. Indeed, some of our black friends here in Harare strongly advised against going.
> Last Friday, 12th May, I was reading a biography of Hudson Taylor and God spoke forcibly to me on the phrase "Advancing Always". He said the first offerings for the Tabernacle, i.e. the dwelling place of God in the Old Testament, were oxen and carts for the transportation of the Tabernacle. This means that the work of God does not stand

still but it is 'always advancing'. Hallelujah. We took this as a word from the Lord and went out on that word.

God truly answered and upheld our faith and we went forward mightily in His name. During the five days we had the joy and privilege of teaching the Word of God to more than six thousand children and their teachers. The listening was phenomenal and the greeting and encouragement really blessed and touched our hearts. Truly God was with us.

"You have blessed us by coming," was a common welcome. They truly blessed us by coming to the Lord in droves. In every school we gave an invitation to receive Christ as Saviour the Holy Spirit was doing His own mighty work. We had the joy of leading five thousand children to the Lord. Hallelujah! To God be all the glory.

There is an openness and desire for God in this country like I have never experienced anywhere else in the ministry. This nation is in dire straits but God is in control and building His kingdom and no one can stop it. Amen

We will be taking our new Correspondence Courses with us next visit and all the children will be using it through the schools. Indeed, it will be part of the school curriculum. We give thanks to God for a safe week. There were some very naughty things happening to white farmers while we were in the district but God kept us safe. Praise the Lord!

Please pray for next Monday 22nd May, which is a big day for us. We are meeting the Social Welfare people regarding fostering a little black girl from one of the orphanages we teach in. Pray we will have favour with this man and there will be no racial overtones.

In the afternoon we have an important meeting with another man regarding the possibility of us teaching literally thousands of Aids orphans in different parts of the country, please pray for these two events. Also, pray for our weekly ministry in Harare Children's Orphanage, the Matthew Rusike Orphanage, the Lovemore Street Kids' Home,

Tyndale PS, Ruwa GNC, Ambassadors for Christ Bible College and the street kids on Tuesday evenings. We are very happy here and feel under no immediate threat in Harare. Pray for our safety. Our car was broken into last week and two cameras were stolen - by some of the street kids.

On one occasion Alan and a team were stopped in the bush by the feared "war veterans". They surrounded the vehicle and started chanting political slogans while threatening to assault or even kill Alan and the team. Another group of war veterans killed a white farmer later that same day. During their chants Alan was praying and finally jumped out of the truck and through an interpreter, he began to preach the gospel to the would-be assassins. He then distributed Every Home Crusade literature to each of the war veterans. They not only grasped for every tract, they were practically fighting each other to make sure they got one. Over one hundred and twenty tracts were put into the hands of these soldiers.

Consequently, the CEF team was released and some of the rebels were born again. All the team felt that the Every Home Crusade literature had been the means God used along with His protecting angels to save their lives.

Sadly, the worsening political agitation interrupted the CEF outreach in the bush and it became too dangerous for Alan and Dorothy to continue working there. The work was delegated to others who lived in these areas while Alan and Dorothy moved into Harare.

The ministry in the city developed very quickly. In just a few years they have trained over two thousand five hundred people in the Christian Leadership courses who are reaching over thirty thousand children each week. Besides the Good News Clubs, Five Day clubs and camps, they work and network with other agencies who are involved in social outreach to the poor areas of Zimbabwe. Presently CEF Zimbabwe is maintaining nine orphanages in different parts of Zimbabwe, providing meals for three thousand children each day and paying the school fees for one thousand five hundred.

The literature ministry is playing a large part in this super-effective ministry in Zimbabwe and Alan expressed his gratitude to the team at the Every Home Crusade factory in a recent letter,

> We praise God for our friends Every Home Crusade in Belfast. We are eagerly awaiting 500,000 children's Tracts, kindly donated by Every Home Crusade in Belfast and just today we have been trying to get Customs to clear them duty free. This is taking longer than expected but we really need their go ahead for a free entry of this literature. We are trusting in God and we believe it will happen soon. We have also been checking out Correspondence Courses for follow up to the tracts and ask you to pray that we will get the best course for these dear children, to help them learn more of our great God.
>
> We went to give Samaritans Purse boxes out in the bush and in three days gave 7000 to needy and very poor children. What an amazing time we had! Children in USA fill shoe boxes with toys, clothes and sweets. The children in Zimbabwe have never and will never get anything like this again. The children did not know what a yo-yo was, nor had they ever seen a jig saw.
>
> We believe this is the beginning of a great wave of God's Spirit in places where white men are still seen as the boss. We are breaking down barriers and God is doing amazing things. Many, many children and adults are being saved as a result of these outreaches.
>
> We also gave some boxes to the children at one of our street kid homes and as a result our photos were in the largest newspaper in Zimbabwe. We pray this will give us more exposure and that people will be interested in what we are doing and want to get involved.
>
> We conducted a training course in Child Evangelism and Children's Ministry on two Saturdays for one hundred and thirty adults and then another one hundred and fifty people

who came from twenty-one different denominations. Praise God, He is using us in a great way to reconcile the people of God in colour issues and cultural differences.

We travelled four hundred kilometres to Mutare, the third biggest town in Zimbabwe, where we trained six groups in Child Evangelism. A few Good News Clubs will start as a result of this effort. No one had ever heard of children's ministry there until this trip and we have been invited back to train all the churches in the city and surrounding areas.

A new door has opened for us to lecture on Child Evangelism in a Bible College on Tuesday morning for two hours each week for thirteen weeks. The principal said he had been praying for years for someone to come and teach this so we are very excited and not a little apprehensive. Please pray for this opening that it will be profitable for the students and us, and that we may even see someone who will catch the vision for CEF and come alongside and join our team. Amen!

Alan and Dorothy still love Zimbabwe and the Lord has provided them with a dedicated team of workers. Two ladies, Jessica Chapfiwa and Perpetual Denga, work full time with them in Harare and the National Director and his wife work in Matabeleland which is in the south of Zimbabwe.

God has honoured the Graham family in their step of faith into Africa. While Alan and Dorothy are enjoying the work in Zimbabwe, daughter Mandy and her husband Darren are in charge of the children's ministry at their local church in Belfast. Gary and his wife Suzanne also lead up the children's ministry in their church. Last but not least, Alan and Dorothy are the proud grandparents of little Daniel who has just celebrated his first birthday – and he is greatly missed by them.

The Every Home Crusade is glad to identify with this industrious team in Zimbabwe and provide the literature that continues to impact the lives of many in that country.

# 8

# TAKING THE WORD IN AND GETTING THE WORD OUT
*with*
*Sid and Jean Garland in Nigeria*

It is reported that AIDS kills some six thousand people each day in Africa - more than wars, famines and floods. Millions of children are orphans, many more live with HIV or AIDS. Nigeria, which justifies the name of "The Giant of Africa" with a population of over 125 million, is under particular threat. It is reckoned that without significant behavioural change 75 million Nigerians will be infected with HIV by the year 2020.

Sid and Jean Garland, missionaries with Mission Africa (formerly Qua Iboe Fellowship), are working at the Theological College of Northern Nigeria. While Sid lectures and directs a literature programme, Jean uses her medical skills to help and encourage people living with HIV/AIDS, teaches about prevention of HIV/AIDS, and helps supervise a programme which administers anti-retro viral drugs especially for children living with the AIDS virus. She sent the following touching report of a young man at the end stages of his life:

> The hospital ward is stifling and confined. In the corner, the thin dark outline of a man lies motionless on the top of a bed, a piece of half-eaten bread on his chest. His upper body moves rapidly up and down as he gasps for air. The effort creates a hustling sound. His mouth is parched and bread crumbs stick to his chopped lips. His black skin is hot to my touch.
>
> This gaunt and almost unrecognizable figure is Adamu and he is my treasured friend. He is a gentle young man, and an intense thinker. He has a degree in theology and in better days liked to preach the gospel and lead others to Jesus Christ. Today Adamu is dying from AIDS. He does not know how he became infected with the AIDS virus, known as HIV. He knows he never had sex before his marriage. Maybe it was from an infected injection needle. God alone knows. What difference does it make anyway?
>
> However, Adamu's friends and the church community do not want to consider that issue. In their eyes, Adamu has AIDS so must be a terrible sinner and they feel justified in not going near him. In their warped minds they feel, and sometimes voice the opinion, that Adamu has brought shame on the church and on Jesus Christ. Like the Pharisees, they feel superior to Adamu and thank God that they are not like him. Adamu lost his job in one church when they discovered he was HIV positive. Then another church employed him, but the people also heard the whispers of AIDS, and they also dismissed him. Even his close family has discarded him. They do not come to visit or to deal with hospital bills. His uncle tells him that he has brought disgrace on the family, and has disappointed their expectations of him.
>
> And here he lies on the hospital bed, his body weak and thin from the constant bouts of diarrhoea and fever. He grasps my hand and whispers, "There is no one here to sing."

I bow closer to him to hear his barely audible words again. "No one has come to sing." This man is dying alone. In the Nigerian culture, especially within the church setting, when a person is sick, others will come and minister to him/her. They will often sing to give spiritual encouragement. So when a believer dies alone, it is significantly tragic, and speaks of rejection by the church. No one from the church should have to die alone. *Dear God, what has happened in Africa that allows people to die alone? What has happened to the church in Nigeria that allows believers to die alone?*

I feel anger at AIDS, the robber of life, health, hope and reputation. I abhor how it has destroyed Adamu's life. I feel overwhelming distress with him for how others have reviled him. My heart breaks for him. I feel such sorrow that those who call themselves Christians do not understand the gospel of grace. Do they not know that none of us deserves God's mercy? Do they not know that we are all sinners, whether we have AIDS or not? Do they not understand that all of us deserve hell? I want to tell them that only faith in the death of Christ can save any of us. How can they reject my friend even if he got AIDS from a sinful act? Are they any better than him? I know I am not. "God be merciful to me, a sinner."

My eyes sting with tears. With faltering words, I remind Adamu of his Saviour who also was despised and rejected by men, a man of sorrows and acquainted with grief. I assure Adamu that Jesus took our sins and our sorrows on him when he died for us. I am greatly comforted that Adamu knows Jesus. There is nothing else I can offer Adamu but Jesus. But what else does a dying man need?

I read from Romans 8, and assure Adamu that there is nothing that can separate him from the love of Christ. "What shall we then say to these things? If God be for us, who can be against us? He that spared not his own Son, but delivered him up for us all, how shall he not with him also freely give us all things? Who shall lay any thing to the charge of God's elect? It is God that justifieth. Who is he that condemneth? It is

Christ that died, yea rather, that is risen again, who is even at the right hand of God, who also maketh intercession for us. Who shall separate us from the love of Christ? shall tribulation, or distress, or persecution, or famine, or nakedness, or peril, or sword? As it is written, For thy sake are we killed all the day long; we are accounted as sheep for the slaughter. Nay, in all these things we are more than conquerors through him that loved us. For I am persuaded, that neither death, nor life, nor angels, nor principalities, nor powers, nor things present, nor things to come, Nor height, nor depth, nor any other creature, shall separate us from the love of God, which is in Christ Jesus our Lord.' (Romans 8:31-39).

His sad eyes look up at me again. "Please write those verses out for me so that I can read them again and again," he whispers.

I will do that. But I doubt if Adamu will be here tomorrow to read them. He will be safe with Jesus in heaven, a place of no more pain. A place where he will be complete, perfect, and able to rejoice once again. Adamu's health improved again, but he died four months later. His wife told me that he asked her every day to read aloud the verses from Romans 8. He would often repeat the verses to himself. Over and over he would say to her, "See my dear wife, even this AIDS has not separated us from Jesus love."

It is a long way from Northern Ireland to northern Nigeria. How did the Garlands come to be involved in this work? Perhaps, the best answer is that of the apostle Paul, "It is God which worketh in you both to will and to do of his good pleasure" (Philippians 2:13). God certainly has been at work in Sid and Jean Garland's lives.

Jean writes:

When I was growing up I learned something very important. Missionaries are not necessarily out of the ordinary, super-spiritual people who hear from God in a way that regular mortals don't, nor do they necessarily have great insights not shared by the usual young person who knows Jesus Christ as Saviour. And how did I learn this? Rarely did a few months pass in our home near Templepatrick, when, as a young person, we did not have these rare creatures, called missionaries, stay in our home. And as I got to know them I found out they were 'normal!' That was one of the first steps in God's preparation of my life for work overseas. From recent conversations with friends I have learned that even yet it would seem that many say to God, "I can't be a missionary. I am not an exceptional person. What could I do for God?"

By God's grace, among our own family circle, we had missionaries in India, China, and Japan, and my mother was prayer secretary to others in Liberia, so I grew up hearing about mission work in Asia and Africa.

I had given my life to Jesus as a very small girl. It was at a point when my mother read me the story of Jesus dying on the cross for my sins. Like many young people brought up in a Christian home, that early decision was repeated several times as a teenager, as I sometimes doubted that I was really His child. I wanted to make my parents' faith my very own. Many times I offered my life to God for His use, and told God that if He wanted me to go overseas to serve Him, I would be willing to do that too. It was partly with this in mind that I decided to be a nurse, much to the displeasure of my headmaster, who voiced the opinion that "Nursing is only something you do if you do not make it to university!" The decision to follow a nursing career is one that I will never regret as the practical training has been so valuable in different areas where I have worked.

Before my 21st birthday I met Sidney Garland, and four months later we knew that we would one day be married and serving God together. Those were exhilarating, heady days. We were both young, but our fervour for God, eagerness for mission, and love for each other were sweet delights that we shared. We both had a great excitement about what God could do for us and through us. Sid headed off to Westminster Seminary for two years, while I finished my general nursing training, a psychiatric course and my midwifery training. We were married in Lylehill Presbyterian Church in 1976 when we were both twenty-three years of age, and I joined Sidney in Philadelphia. I worked as a nurse while he finished his M.Div. and started his MTh. Unknown to us then, getting to know America and how Americans think was part of God's preparation for life in Nigeria, as our children would eventually go to an American school in Nigeria, and Debbie would go to an American university. We grew to appreciate Americans and their efficient, meticulous way of doing things.

After Sidney graduated from Westminster, we came back to Belfast, and he was installed as minister of Finaghy Evangelical Presbyterian Church. The people of Finaghy were long-suffering with their young inexperienced pastor and the inexpert pastor's wife as we endeavoured to serve them for nine years. Peter, Debbie and Anna were born during that time. In those years, God also give us the opportunity to serve with LIFE, the pro-life, anti-abortion group. In fact we started the group in Northern Ireland. I now see this work as part of His preparation time for me to learn the counselling and communication skills needed to help young people in very difficult situations. I am still using those skills in Nigeria within the AIDS programmes that I work for. God does not make mistakes. Nothing in our life is wasted if we let Him use it.

In 1986 God began to speak to us about serving him overseas. Those were exhilarating days as we scrutinized and prayed about various openings for service. The life and ministry of Rev. Bill Leach prompted us to think about Qua Iboe and Nigeria. Taking courage, and being persuaded that God was leading us, we applied to Qua Iboe Fellowship to go to

Samuel Bill Theological College for only a two year period. Sidney would teach young men training for the pastoral ministry, and I would teach our three children. Looking back on those decision making days now, it was a considerable step to pull the children out of Finaghy Primary School, pack up, let our house, and head off to the bush of South East Nigeria.

For the next two years we experienced and absorbed Nigerian church life in SBTC, Abak, in Cross River State, (now Akwa Ibom State). Sid never failed to come home from the classroom full of enthusiasm at the honour of teaching his students. They were so prepared to be trained. I established a small classroom in an empty house on our compound and each weekday the three children and I went to school from 8 am. until noon. Dealing with the sweltering muggy climate proved to be one of my biggest hurdles. In the classroom my three pupils would have no shirts on, and the condensation would build up on their backs by 10am. Pencils would slip from their hands, and they would wilt half way through the morning. We dealt with this problem by going out and buying a small portable generator that ran a fan. That was one of the best decisions we made. Moving air in the classroom helped the teacher have increased staying power, and her three small students deliberate better. When not in school the children loved African life. They ran barefoot with their Nigerian friends, climbing and naming trees, burying each other in the dark mud, and making up imaginative dramas. They were extremely happy and apart from malaria now and then, very healthy.

In the afternoons, I used my nursing skills to run a small dispensary for the theological students. This way I got to know them and to pray for and with them when they were ill. Learning how to run a home in this remote corner of Nigeria was a challenge. It took me most of the first two years to learn how to make good yeast bread, and develop recipes using local foods. We all lost weight which for me was no bad thing!

As the two years passed in Nigeria, God spoke to us about staying longer. A Nigerian missionary leader, called Bayo Feminure spoke at a mission's conference at Abak. As he told us of the many millions in Nigeria who have never heard about Jesus, we both felt that God was speaking to us. From the vantage point of Abak, when we looked at Northern Ireland, the comfortable and materially undemanding lifestyle, the many evangelical churches and the opportunities for Christian teaching every night of the week, we were moved with compassion for the millions who have never had the opportunity to know Jesus Christ, nor the opportunity to be taught the Bible. Like many before us, Africa had invaded our hearts.

After furlough, we moved back to Nigeria and to about 500 miles further north from Abak, to Bukuru and the Theological College of Northern Nigeria (TCNN). This meant that Sid could continue to teach theology, and mission, and that the children could now go to Hillcrest School, Jos, which would help prepare them academically for life ahead. I had been running out of ideas on how to teach Peter. He was ten years old and needed better teachers than me and all three needed the competition and social stimulus of a school. We have been very privileged to have our children live with us in Nigeria. Many of their friends were boarders at Hillcrest. All three have received a wonderful education at this American mission school, having opportunities for sports, drama, music as well as a wide general education. All three are now university graduates: Peter in medicine, Debbie in nursing, and Anna in psychology.

Meanwhile, God opened doors for me to serve him in Bukuru too. Our home became a hospitality centre for many. God gave me two good helpers in the house who have been with us now for the past eleven years. These ladies, Dorcas and

Angelina, have learned to clean and cook and have allowed me time and energy to work outside the home. We make our own bread, cakes, biscuits, yogurt, breakfast cereals, sauces, etc. Food preparation takes so much longer than in Northern Ireland, and the dust and dirt on the concrete floors needs daily attention.

At TCNN, I supervised a Primary Health Clinic which served the college community and the surrounding area. It is a busy place. I also led a women's Bible Study group for 8 years under the umbrella of Bible Study Fellowship. The opportunities for fellowship and learning with Nigerian women during those studies have been the nearest that I have ever been to heaven on earth. I have often been in sharing times with Nigerian women and have just not wanted them to stop. Many times I have wished that I could transport my friends from Northern Ireland to Nigeria to sit in on those precious times.

In the year 2000, we moved from Bukuru to Jos, which is twelve miles further north. A combination of my nursing training, experience of working with LIFE in Northern Ireland, learning in the medical field in Nigeria, getting to know and understand some of Nigerian culture, and a compassion that comes from Christ himself, have helped me to minister into the crisis of AIDS in Nigeria.

I have been working with several different AIDS ministries in Nigeria. I was asked to work with Fellowship of Christian Students, which is affiliated to Scripture Union, Africa. My job with them has entailed a lot of travelling and training others, e.g. pastors, teachers and youth workers, to do AIDS education for those in their care. This involves training in the facts about AIDS, how to avoid it, and how to care for and counsel those living with HIV/AIDS. But it also involves training young people in life skills, based on God's word, so that they will not be in danger from AIDS. As many as two out of every ten young people in Nigeria are dying from

AIDS and need to know Jesus. It is hard for us in Northern Ireland to imagine the scale of the problem faced by the African church. AIDS is an issue that almost every pastor and extended family deals with frequently. Personally I have several friends dying from AIDS.

Other AIDS ministries involve co-writing AIDS curriculum for the Federal Government of Nigeria. This is for use by Primary and Secondary school Christian Religious Knowledge teachers. I also have the opportunity to serve on the AIDS ministry supervisory committees for two major denominations in Nigeria. God giving me the ability to write booklets about AIDS for use by young people seems to have proved beneficial to many.

Jos is at the interface between the predominately Muslim north of Nigeria and the predominantly Christian south. Militant Islam, in its endeavour to impose Muslim law on Nigeria, has been pushing south. This has led to recent civil unrest with much death and destruction in Jos and other communities in northern Nigeria. But this has also been a time to emphasize the truths of the Christian faith which teach us to love others, and a time for Islam to be exposed as a religion which is devoid of real love and hope.

Each time we return to Northern Ireland we are saddened by how western culture is rapidly slipping further and further away from Biblical standards. We are also saddened that many, even within our churches, have little concern for those in developing countries who are poor, have few opportunities for good health and education, and may have never heard of the love of Christ. We long for more people from Northern Ireland to actually go out to other parts of the world which are so needy. When Jesus told us to go into all the world, he did envisage us getting out of our comfort zones and going somewhere else.

My testimony is overwhelmingly one of God's provision for us and goodness to us. We do not feel that our lives to this point have been times of hardship, loss and deprivation. True, we and our children have had our struggles, especially with separation from each other, sickness, and adjustment to other cultures. But he has given us the joy of rewarding service, and the delight of seeing others come to faith in Him. He has given us the crises from time to time that have caused us to lean back on Him and helped us to prove that even in sickness or loneliness, God is totally good. As we have stepped out in obedience to Him, He has provided for our needs in every area. As a family, we often literally laugh out loud at God's goodness to us as we prove over and over that when we repeatedly give to others, both in monetary terms and materially, God just keeps giving even more back to us. Our children have a world view that is much wider than if they had been raised in Northern Ireland. They appreciate other cultures and they love the Lord, and desire to keep serving Him too. By God's grace, I want to continue to serve the purpose of God in my generation. I want to continue to give my life for something that will last forever. May God help me to do this.

Sid Garland was not only born into a Christian home; he was a son of the manse. His arrival was quite precarious because his mother, Mrs. Maisie Garland, was seriously ill in a Belfast hospital for more than a week following the difficult delivery of her eleven-pound baby boy on July 25th 1952. Rev. Charles Haddon Garland, Sid's father, was a minister of the Irish Evangelical Church, now the Evangelical Presbyterian Church. As an only child Sid was privileged to enjoy a loving Christian home surrounded by many encouragements, prayers, and of course, Christian literature. Sometimes as a boy young Sid did not appreciate these benefits and felt the burden of being a minister's son. The dubious privilege often invited mocking from peers outside the home and some unwise expectations from within the Christian family. For a long time he resisted and resented the frequent comment, "You will follow in your father's footsteps."

Like many other children in Christian homes during the fifties, Sid was brought up on Vos's *Child's Story Bible*, He realized from his earliest days that belonging to a Christian family did not make him acceptable in God's sight. At the tender age of five, Sid asked God to forgive the wrong things in his life and to be his Saviour and Friend. The conversion experience happened at a Sunday School class in a very small rural church in Clintyfallow, Country Tyrone. Audrey McNeill, who was Sid's Sunday School teacher at the time, later married Paul Reid and they have been missionaries for many years with CEF Europe.

Youth leaders, books, camps and involvement in children's ministry all played a part in helping Sid to stand firm in his faith. One person who was a particular inspiration in young Sid Garland's life was the late Rev. W. J. Grier, early father of the Irish Evangelical Church. Sid never forgot his warm-hearted personal encouragement, zealous preaching, and passionate prayers. Rev. Grier's convictions on the importance of books and publishing left a lasting mark on the young man's life.

Alongside his pastoral ministry in Botanic Avenue Evangelical Presbyterian Church (EPC), the Reverend Grier was committed to literature ministry. This was expressed through the Evangelical Bookshop which was situated opposite the school Sid attended, the Evangelical magazine, book and tract writing, and the encouragement he gave to new publishers such as Evangelical Press and the Banner of Truth Trust. The Reverend Grier delighted to review and recommend good books to God's people and especially young men. One book that Sid greatly benefited from was Rev. Grier's wonderful little book about books, Best Books.

Sid attended the Royal Belfast Academical Institution for his secondary education and while there he had the privilege of hearing many outstanding evangelical speakers at the Inst. Christian Union and at the weekly Torchbearers meeting in Belfast YMCA which was nearby. It was at Torchbearers that Sid first met the special girl he would later marry, Jean Rea.

When Sid enrolled at Queen's University in Belfast he enjoyed the leadership training which he received through the University's Christian Union (CU). In retrospect, Sid recognises the significant force for good that was brought about on his life by the CU's emphasis on bookstalls, book reviews and the importance of reading. Some books like Packer's Knowing God, gripped his heart and mind. Through his Hebrew classes he also had contact with many students for the Presbyterian ministry and Sid saw the important role of the Evangelical Bookshop in countering Liberalism and promoting the Evangelical and Reformed faith. Many of the key books, which Sid found helpful, originated from the faculty of Westminster Seminary.

In 1974, after graduating from Queen's University, Sid crossed the Atlantic to the beautiful city of Philadelphia where he began a post graduate course at Westminster Theological Seminary. Sid chose Westminster with the expectation that it was the best seminary he could find in the whole world, and he was not disappointed. Sid says of those days, "I will always be grateful for the wonderful grounding I received there. Westminster provided me with the ability to critique anything I came across in the light of the Scriptures. One of the lasting inspirations was the Westminster Bookstore which worked hand in hand with the professors to get the books needed for the respective classes. The bookstore also helped students build their own library for a lifetime of service."

During Sid's final year at Queen's he again met up with, and this time fell in love with, Jean Rea whom he had previously met at Torchbearers. When Sid told Jean of his plan to go for further studies in Philadelphia her heart sank. However, God confirmed to both of them that they were meant for each other. Sid and Jean painstakingly endured the separation of those two years during which time Jean completed her nursing and midwifery training in Belfast. Travel and communication were more difficult at that time, but love always finds a way and for those two years the sweethearts exchanged letters across the Atlantic six days every week.

Finally, on June 18th 1976 the joyful day arrived when Sid and Jean were married in Lylehill Presbyterian Church. Rev. W. J. Grier was invited to preach the sermon at the marriage service and he based it on John 1:16. "And of his fullness have all we received, and grace for grace" (KJV) or as the ESV puts it "grace upon grace". Truly their life together since that day has been a story of grace upon grace.

Missionary interest started for Sid and Jean when they were young. During those formative years there were ample opportunities not only to hear missionaries speak, but also to interact with them in their homes. All this made a significant impact. Sid showed a keen interest in several missionary societies and their literature was carefully set out in his bedroom on a chest of drawers. Little tin boxes sat on top of each pile of magazines or prayer letters and into these he put small amounts from his pocket money. Periodically he sent the money to the appropriate missionary society and was greatly encouraged to receive letters back. It made young Sid feel he was involved with the missionaries. The Free Church of Scotland Missions (India, South Africa and Peru), European Missionary Fellowship, Overseas Missionary Fellowship, Child Evangelism Fellowship, Christian Witness to Israel and the Africa Inland Mission, were among the various areas of interest that captivated and motivated Sid.

When the Reverend Joe and Mrs. McCracken, who were serving the Lord in South Africa, visited Belfast in 1964 they spoke at Somerton Road EPC. After the service Sid told them that he felt the Lord leading him to give his life for missionary service. Sid was only twelve years of age at that time.

Missionary biographies also played a very important role in encouraging the young man's zeal for missions. He still remembers the impact these books made on his life: The Three Freds, David Livingstone, Hudson Taylor, Through Gates of Splendour, Jungle Pilot, and later Five Pioneer Missionaries.

After graduation from Westminster 1977, Sid and Jean returned to Belfast with a sense of being missionaries to Ireland. Sid was very impatient to begin his pastoral ministry. However, the Lord had other plans and for a period He put Sid to work under John Grier in the

Evangelical Bookshop. A few months later, he accepted a pastoral call and was ordained and installed as minister of Finaghy Evangelical Presbyterian Church in South Belfast on April 7th 1978.

Their early experiences in the ministry included a work done by God which saw a number of young people coming to faith in Christ. During that time Sid was conscious that they were reaping a harvest where his cousin and predecessor, Rev. Norman Reid, now a missionary in South Africa, had laboured. As is often the experience, there were both encouragements and discouragements over those years working with the group of young people and youth workers, but Sid and Jean are thankful that some of those same young people continue to go on strong in their Christian faith.

The "Troubles" in Northern Ireland were still very bad during Sid and Jean's time at Finaghy, but having a Reformed world and life view, they were filled with confidence that the gospel would have an impact, not only on individuals, but on the whole of culture, community life and politics. While at Westminster Seminary Sid had opportunity to listen to Dr. Francis Schaeffer and Dr. C. Everett Koop, who later became the Surgeon General of the USA. The Schaeffer & Koop book and film series by the title, *Whatever Happened to the Human Race?* played a part in motivating Sid and Jean to establish the pro-life group, LIFE (Northern Ireland) and also with John Ling, Evangelicals for LIFE. One influential book at that time was entitled, Using the Media. It gave a lot of practical guidance on how to get a message across to many people. Jean did most of the public speaking for LIFE, while Sid was involved in leadership and literature production. During this venture both Sid and Jean acquired skills which have continued to be useful in Africa.

Working in south Belfast convinced Sid and Jean that Northern Ireland is one of the most privileged places in the world. They reckoned that even if their local church did not exist, the church members would be able to attend any one of four other evangelical churches within walking distance. During their time at Finaghy EPC Rev. Bill Leach and several missionaries from the Qua Iboe Fellowship, now Mission Africa, visited the church. Sid and Jean were earnestly praying that God would call someone from their church to this work. They were shocked to discover later that God answered their prayers and called them.

One of Sid's favourite Westminster professors was Harvie Conn. Harvie had been a missionary to Korea. His ministry among the commercial sex workers of Korean cities combined social concern with the transforming power of the gospel. It was a great privilege for Sid and Jean when Harvie consented to preach at their Farewell Service on the eve of their departure for Nigeria in 1987.

The excitement of a new challenge and culture only masked the fear and trepidation that Sid and Jean felt as they left Northern Ireland for Nigeria along with their three children, Peter then seven years old, Debbie five, and Anna who was only three years old.

Settling in to a new way of life in a different climate and culture called for many adjustments. It was not easy for Jean particularly. Besides having to care for the family with all the dangers and difficulties of the new environment, she also had the challenge of home schooling the children. With the Lord's help, Jean was greatly encouraged in this. She did very well at the teaching, the children were happy with their new life, and Sid enjoyed his new role as a lecturer.

One hundred years earlier, in 1887, Samuel Bill had gone out from Belfast to Nigeria as a missionary. His life, dedication and ministry resulted in a Qua Iboe denomination which developed into more than 1200 congregations. For Sid and Jean it was encouraging for them to see the hunger for God's Word in those congregations and at the Samuel Bill Theological College (SBTC) where they worked. They fitted in well with the faculty and Sid was very happy to be now part of a team after the rather solitary pressures of the traditional 'one man ministry' in the church at home.

An early surprise for the Garland family was how readily the people accepted church services of four hours or more. However, Sid and Jean also became conscious that there was still a lot of need for teaching, evangelism and even pioneer mission work in unreached areas. Today Sid and Jean can still vividly recall their early reactions to the sight of traditional shrines and carved images. Their encounters with these fetish objects of worship and superstition made them keenly aware of a heavy atmosphere of darkness and evil. Sid was particularly disturbed and challenged by discovering a large quantity of beautifully produced literature from the Jehovah's Witnesses in a very poor home. This motivated him further to provide teaching and literature that would feed the minds of African pastors, teachers and missionaries.

The students often came pleading with the teacher for help to obtain good literature. Some colleagues brought discouragements, saying that this was the responsibility of the church, or by saying that Nigerians could not afford books. Low incomes and the devaluation of Nigeria's currency were certainly obstacles to placing valuable reading material in their hands. However, one colleague, Martin Bussey, was prepared to supply the small college bookstore with good books and Sid and his friends were surprised to see that the Nigerians were prepared to save and sacrifice in order to better equip themselves for the ministry. Sid's partnership with Martin Bussey in bringing books to Africa has continued even though Martin now serves the Lord in Nairobi, Kenya.

It is difficult to live in tropical Africa and escape many of the maladies that frequently afflict the population. The Garlands have had their own health battles with malaria, boils and infected prickly heat rashes. They had to learn how to survive in a hot steamy climate and to do without many of the luxuries of the western world. One particularly stressful time was when they were issued with a repatriation order from the immigration authorities. They were advised by the church's barrister to leave the state and present their case in the Federal capital, Abuja. This meant a nerve-wracking trip across the state border, hoping that they would not be stopped by the immigration authorities who were normally on duty there. Assured of the prayers of their colleagues the Garland family were able to make their escape, and received a favourable hearing in Abuja. When Jean's sister's baby died of a cot death, news did not reach them for six weeks. Poor communications highlighted the frustration of being so cut off from family in those days.

Originally, Sid, Jean and the family only went to Nigeria for a two-year term. They had no idea how they or their three small children would cope. In answer to prayer they soon settled into the work and busy routine. Jean was busy with the home-schooling programme and the children were very happy. Before the two years were up, they felt the Lord was telling them they should return to Nigeria after a short spell at home in Northern Ireland. They were particularly excited by the increasing willingness of Nigerians to take up the unfinished task of reaching the unreached inside their own country.

Sid and Jean's primary plan was to return to SBTC after the short home assignment, but due to health problems in one of their children, they were seconded to Action Partners (SUM) and were assigned to teach at the Theological College of Northern Nigeria (TCNN), near Jos. However, the family had a very rough initiation into their new assignment when their ten year-old son, Peter, became gravely ill and was near to death before he was being stretchered out of Nigeria and straight into theatre at the Royal Belfast Hospital for Sick Children. It was a very anxious time for the family and Peter bravely suffered so much pain. It was very tough for Jean to watch his suffering and slow recovery in hospital. It was also difficult for Sid who remained in Nigeria with the two girls.

Eventually the prayers of many people were answered and three months after their sudden evacuation, Peter and Jean were able to return to Nigeria. Locally in Nigeria the story is told of a crazy white man waving excitedly from the rooftop railings at Kano Airport as the returnees touched down on Nigerian soil..

In the Garland's prayer letter after following this event, after experience of the sustaining grace of God, Sid quoted the words of David Livingstone:

*Lord, send me anywhere - Only go with me.*
*Lay any burden on me, - Only sustain me.*
*Sever any tie - But the tie that binds me to Thyself.*

The Theological College of Northern Nigeria is one of the leading theological seminaries in Nigeria. TCNN not only trains pastors, teachers and the top leadership levels of the church, but also, those who in turn will be training others for the ministry. It was very encouraging for Sid and Jean to be able to remain long enough in Nigeria to see their students occupying key positions as missionaries, bishops, lecturers and even principals.

On his first arrival at TCNN Sid was appointed to the Library Committee. Already the need for a new library had been recognized to enable the college to start its Master's programme. This meant that Sid was immediately involved in ordering library supplies and especially books. About nine months later after their arrival they had the joy of opening the new library. Meanwhile, in an early prayer letter from Jos (January 1991) Sid was clearly burdened by the fact that their students were starved of books - "these are often unaffordable or are simply not available." This burden caused Sid to think and pray about how best to meet this need.

In 1991 Sid began a four-year period as Deputy Provost of TCNN. A year later, alongside his Nigerian colleagues, he became involved in a battle to uphold Biblical doctrinal standards at the College. As a result, the TCNN Board asked an American missionary lecturer to leave the college because of his liberal teaching. Because of the strong stand of the Board in defence of its evangelical basis of faith, another missionary couple from Germany also left the college. Sid counted it a privilege to be able to encourage the Nigerian churches to take their stand on the truth of God's Word.

This proved to be a difficult period for Sid and Jean, with furious accusations being made against them. Nevertheless, in spite of the antagonism, they were very sure that this was a crucial time for the future direction of TCNN. They could also see the importance of sound theological books which defend the integrity of the Word of God and contradict attacks on the evangelical faith.

By September 1991, Sid, with help from Martin Bussey, started to bring books into the College. Early bookselling operations began in the afternoons from the Garland's house. That same year, Africa Christian Textbooks (ACTS) began to take shape as a group of lecturers from different Bible colleges got together and shared their frustrations at not having textbooks and other books for their students.

In 1993, in the providence of God, TCNN asked ACTS to provide a bookshop at TCNN. The bookshop got off the ground with part-time student help, but has now grown to over twenty staff. Although Sid and Jean are very grateful for important financial support, including the key seed money from Tearfund, as well as from Mission Africa, the best thing the Lord has done for them is the team of people He has provided for them.

Sid feels particularly blessed to have someone whom he calls his 'right-hand-man.' Rev. Luka Vandi at first was one of their students; then he became a student worker in the bookshop and then the first full-time employee at the bookshop. With the steady growth of ACTS, the Reverend Luka Vandi has been a great asset to the work. He is knowledgeable, hard-working and faithful to the vision of ACTS. His tall stature and broad smile are impressive, but even more so is the way he welcomes customers and talks excitedly about the books that are now available.

Other missionaries have joined Sid and Jean to help in the progress of the ACTS work. Ken and Anne Mizon came to them through Action Partners. It was a mysterious providence when they had to leave Nigeria a short time later due to Anne needing treatment for cancer. However, Sid and Jean kept in touch with the Mizons and they have been able to return to Africa, specifically to Uganda with the Tools for the Job project of Africa Inland Mission. God has sent other workers to Sid and Jean to help in the administration of ACTS, including Pamela Johnston from Northern Ireland.

During these years in Nigeria Sid was able to work on his doctorate. Professor Harvie Conn was his advisor. Sid obtained his Doctor of Ministry in Urban Mission project on "Teaching Missiology at TCNN" in 1997.

Sid and Jean have been burdened by the lack of good books in the churches, and especially in their theological colleges and mission training schools all across Nigeria, and beyond. Sid's concern was to see how they could provide the books at centres closer to those who needed them most. With God's help they were able to open other strategically located ACTS branches. Appropriately one of them is in the college where Sid started out – SBTC. Another centre is in sub-Saharan Africa's largest city, Lagos. Yet another book centre is in the leading Baptist seminary in Ogbomosho. More recently they have been able to open a branch in the Nairobi Evangelical Graduate School of Theology (NEGST). This strategically located shop and distribution centre is managed by none other than their former colleague, Martin Bussey.

Another key development for ACTS has been the way in which literature is provided to help educate concerning HIV/AIDS, and to care for those suffering because AIDS has come to them or their families. Jean's main ministry, especially since the children have left home, has been to work with various groups doing HIV/AIDS education from a Biblical viewpoint. She also helps supervise various compassionate ministries to those living with HIV/AIDS.

Over the last years God has given many international partners to ACTS enabling them to advance their literature ministry. One of the most valued of these is the Every Home Crusade (EHC) from Belfast Northern Ireland. When Sid was growing up he frequently heard Mr. Ernie Allen, the founder of Every Home Crusade and The Revival Movement, preach in various Evangelical Presbyterian Churches. After Sid and Jean arrived in Africa they discovered in the early 1990s that the ministry of ACTS and Every Home Crusade wonderfully dove-tailed together. Although the agencies were different, they had complementary ministries.

Alongside the need to provide reading material for pastors and missionaries to help build and equip them for their work, Sid also appreciates that these same pastors and missionaries are in a great position to make use of literature tools in evangelising those who do not know Christ. For this reason the students and other customers of ACTS need exactly what EHC is able to supply. The ACTS team gladly helps with the storage and distribution of the EHC materials. Through the Garlands, EHC has been able to link with the Fellowship of Christian Students (FCS). The Fellowship of Christian Students is a large student and schools ministry linked to Scripture Union. As well as making use of EHC tracts and Scripture portions, FCS has benefited from the printing of Bible Study materials.

At TCNN and through other contacts, ACTS is in a great position to provide EHC materials to many different denominations and evangelistic ministries. They are also working on getting evangelistic materials translated into other languages and in this relation have linked with a retired SUM missionary, Mrs. Pixie Moles. Pixie is particularly burdened with the need of Africa's largest unreached people group - the nomadic Fulani tribe. Through ACTS, EHC has also printed and shipped language primers to help the church among the Bassa tribe in an area pioneered by Northern Ireland missionary, Robert Hyslop. The New Tribes edition of Bible Pictures which are used for teaching and evangelising children and are printed and provided by EHC, are also now being distributed through ACTS.

In August 1998 Sid wrote to EHC:

Dear Brother Adams,

We are excited that we now have permission to print *The Gospel of John* in the Hausa Language. This would be wonderful for evangelising and soulwinning. Your English *The Gospel of John* is popular here in Nigeria, and is being widely used. However, many people cannot speak English. Hausa is one of the major languages of Nigeria and West Africa. There are probably as many as 40 million persons who speak Hausa in Nigeria. It is also used as a trade language by two hundred smaller tribes in the Northern and middle belt of Nigeria.

Would your Revival Movement, Every Home Crusade, take on the printing of this new *The Gospel of John* in the Hausa language? This gospel would also be used in reaching Moslems in Northern Nigeria. It would be distributed also to about 100 unreached tribes in West Africa, many of whom are very open to receive the gospel message.

If you were to ask us how many you would need to print, the answer would be AS MANY MILLION COPIES AS POSSIBLE. We do not have funds to undertake this work. Meanwhile, I shall look forward to hearing from you about this matter. With gratitude for all your fellowship in the work of the gospel...

While ACTS has helped to distribute EHC materials, they have also benefited greatly from the help EHC has provided in shipping books. A lot of literature was being sent to Nigeria through the Post Office until EHC realized that it would save everybody money by shipping their literature by container. With the support of EHC, and the co-operation of Dr. Ebenezer Obey in Lagos, ACTS has been able to ship thousands of new books from UK publishers, also second hand books, and books donated through the Evangelical bookshop and Langham Literature (Evangelical Literature Trust).

The miracle of getting containers through the Nigerian ports is on-going. One mission group had a container delayed in port for two years after which the mission had to pay so many dollars that they promised never to send a container through a Nigerian port again. The containers from Belfast have experienced delays and losses, but generally God has used Samuel Adams, EHC and their partners in Lagos to have their books safely delivered to ACTS. This has made a very significant contribution to the advancement of the cause of Christ in Nigeria.

Every Home Crusade continues to work through Sid and Jean Garland and their fine team of workers as the following letter indicates:

We are eagerly looking forward to the arrival of the next container of literature. It is good news that its journey has commenced. *The Gospel of John* booklet in Hausa is not only useful in itself but is also an encouragement to those going out for evangelism. Perhaps without these Gospel of John booklets they would not go out at all. I'd say there is a near insatiable demand here, so depending on your budget and priorities we will be needing more in the not too distant future.

We are hearing of more and more Muslim converts, though at the same time the enemy is working to make it more difficult for Muslims to become Christians. One young Muslim was reached by our students. His life was threatened, and he felt he had to leave home. Now he has been baptised and is getting involved in a church. A Christian organization offering help to Muslims who become Christians has employed and housed him.

Some states in Nigeria have introduced Sharia law under which it will be a crime worthy of death for a Muslim to become a Christian. However, God's word is more powerful, and nothing is too hard for the Lord. Thanks again for your partnership in prayer and generous supply of literature.

Sid and Jean continue in the work in Northern Nigeria. From there Sid sent the following:

My excitement about ministry in Nigeria, and especially literature ministry has not changed. I continue to find a thrill in providing our brothers and sisters in Nigeria and other countries in Africa with God's Word and the tools to help them understand it more clearly. Jean and I love working here and pray for many more years of health to continue the ministries God has given us. Our three children are now young adults, but all three see Nigeria as their home. Through God's grace in their lives, they all have a love for the Lord and want to use their lives to serve Him.

Africa is the only continent that is poorer today than it was twenty years ago. Yet the church is still growing faster than on any other continent, and there is a growing vision of what Africa can contribute to the cause of Christ worldwide. One of our ACTS Board of Directors is Timothy Olonade. Timothy has experience in publishing, particularly books related to mission. He is currently the Executive Secretary of the Nigeria Evangelical Missions Association (NEMA). He calculates that currently there are 5,000 Nigerian cross-cultural missionaries, but NEMA have set a target to contribute a work force of 50,000 by 2015 to the mission enterprise of the global church.

An Ulsterman, Lowry Maxwell, was among the pioneers of the Sudan United Mission in 1904. Fifty years later he wrote a book entitled, 'Half a Century of Grace'. It was an apt title. In 2004 the churches that resulted from this work were joyfully celebrating and thanking God for a century of grace. God by His grace has not only preserved the church, but has given remarkable growth. This in spite of recent persecutions which have seen hundreds of churches burned and thousands of Christians killed.

We also gladly acknowledge that it is the grace of God that has made it possible for us to serve in Nigeria. In spite of some hard times, we consider it more a privilege than a sacrifice to be on this field. We have been privileged to take the Word in (throughout out lives) and in turn to get the Word out to so many people. Of course, there have been disappointments with some people. The church has a good deal of nominalism, and the gospel is not always clearly preached. There is need for genuine revival, but God has been gracious to us in so many ways. He has given to us colleagues who have vision and zeal; He has given us students and friends who have been so appreciative of our efforts; He has given us health and strength for the task; and, above all, He has given us a family that are committed to the Lord and to mission.

It is our ambition to go on serving wherever God guides and enables. As one of our pioneer Qua Iboe missionaries used to say, "Who wouldn't be a missionary?"

# 9

## FLOODING THE PHILIPPINES WITH THE GOSPEL
### *Gareth and Lorelei McDowell*

Large cardboard boxes were piled high and dominated every room of the house. They were taking over. The family had to manoeuvre the table and chairs when they would sit down to eat in order to accommodate the stacked-up cartons. To climb into bed at night was an ordeal and required some expertise lest the boxes should come crashing down. Visiting family and friends had to peer around cardboard pillars while exchanging conversation with each other. A stack of boxes in the kitchen rivalled for the much needed working space. Boxes were everywhere.

These boxes, Gareth McDowell assured his understanding and longsuffering in-laws, would soon be gone. Gareth and his wife Lorelei lived in Tarlac, situated in the heartland of the Philippines rich plain of Luzon. They were overjoyed to receive another consignment consisting of ten tonnes of much needed Every Home Crusade literature. It had been delivered to their home on a large lorry from Manila. However, their excitement was moderately tempered with dilemma, for they had no place to store the precious cargo. The warehouse repository for which Gareth and Lorelei had been praying did not materialise. With no repository available, they had no other option than to ask Mr. Cunanan to stockpile the enormous load in his home.

Mr. Cunanan was as excited as the young couple and was only too glad to agree to use his home as a literature store. For years he had prayed that God would use his home and family as a gospel witness in the region, and he felt this was one way they could serve the Lord.

Just as Gareth and Lorelei had predicted, the boxes soon began to disappear. News quickly filtered through to many churches, pastors and evangelists that Gospel of John booklets, Bible portions and tracts from Every Home Crusade in Northern Ireland had arrived in Tarlac. Soon a steady stream of visitors was calling at the Cunanan residence, some as early as 5.30 a.m., to receive their quota of the much-awaited literature.

Within two months all ten tonnes of gospel booklets, evangelistic tracts and Bible material had been dispersed, and Mr. Cunanan saw his home return to normal. For a few days they thought that some form of normality had returned. It was not to last.

Exceptionally heavy monsoon rains swept over Luzon Province causing the Tarlac River which traverses the city, to overflow and cause widespread flooding. The Cunanans' residence and neighbourhood in the San Sebastian Village area of Tarlac were inundated by the swell of murky brown water. The stagnant water which invaded the houses maintained its high level for several days. All moveable furniture had to be elevated on wooden benches. Although the unwelcome flood left Mr. Cunanan bewildered, he wholeheartedly joined Gareth and Lorelei in thanking God that the flood had not arrived in time to damage or destroy the precious printed material from Every Home Crusade. Gareth and Lorelei were sure that people back home in Northern Ireland had been praying for them and their literature mission to the Philippines.

Gareth McDowell, the middle child of one brother and one sister, was born into a Christian home in Dungannon, County Tyrone, Northern Ireland. Being raised in a God-fearing home, church also became a significant part of his young life. Like his brother and sister, Gareth learned hymns, scripture verses and Bible stories at home, in Sunday School and at church, even before he attended day school.

When he was only seven years old Gareth accepted the Lord Jesus Christ as his personal Saviour following a Sunday evening evangelistic service. Rather than wait at the church to speak with the preacher, Gareth confided in his parents at home that he needed to be saved, and his mum and dad, Errol and Noreen McDowell, had great satisfaction in leading their son to a personal knowledge of Jesus Christ.

At that early age neither Gareth nor his parents were aware of the implications of that initial step of receiving Jesus Christ. However, Errol and Noreen had been praying not only for the salvation of their children, but also that God would use them in His work.

During his years at school Gareth identified with other children who acknowledged Jesus Christ as their Saviour. This did not mean that Gareth did not misbehave. Like other children of his age he got up to plenty of boyish mischief, but through it all he never stopped attending church on Sunday. As time allowed he also was present at the mid-week prayer meeting. Even though Gareth was not aware of it, God was evidently at work in his life.

After high school Gareth enrolled at an Electrical College, and after four years he qualified as an approved electrician. It was just after he was fully eligible to earn some serious money that life took an unexpected turn. Even though Gareth never lost his zeal for his Christian life or his church, Mullaglass Free Presbyterian Church, he never thought God would ever ask him to become a preacher or a missionary. He felt totally inadequate for such a step, and therefore, dismissed any possibility of such a calling from his mind and future plans.

However, God had other plans for the young man's life. During the annual Easter Convention at Martyrs' Memorial Church in Belfast,

Dr. Myron Guiler from the Marietta Bible Center Church, Ohio, gave the challenge at the end of the Saturday evening missionary rally. Gareth distinctly heard God speak to him that night and he went forward to the front of the church to surrender his life to Jesus Christ.

Even following that experience at the Easter Convention, Gareth still did not entertain the thought that God would want him to preach. The young man considered himself to be too shy to speak in public. He never had engaged in any public speaking before and he was not about to start.

Several months later Gareth was overtaken by a strange but inescapable conviction that he should go to Bible College to prepare for Christian service. At first he questioned his own sanity, for such a step seemed pointless; there was no way he could ever be a preacher. Nevertheless, in spite of his protests, the persuasive conviction continued until he yielded to God and announced to friends and family that God was calling him to prepare for Christian work.

When Gareth began to contemplate which college he should go to he remembered that in his preaching Dr. Guiler had spoken of the Marrietta Bible College in the United States. Gareth decided he would survey the possibility of enrolling at Marrietta and after a visit to Ohio in 1994 he had no hesitation in making application to the college. He was duly accepted for the four-year pastoral course and left home in Markethill in September 1995 to begin his studies.

The student body at the Marrietta Bible College was quite an international group. There were over sixty students from seven different countries, but Gareth was the only one from the United Kingdom. The senior students who already had overcome any homesickness in previous years soon befriended the British new-comer and helped him settle into his new surroundings.

Amongst those who paid particular attention was Lorelei Cunanan, a beautiful third-year student from Tarlac, in the Philippines. What initially began as friendship blossomed into romance, and Gareth knew that he had fallen in love with this pretty and radiant Filipino girl.

Lorelei had been born in the city of Tarlac, a favourite stopover place between Manila in the south and Baguio in the north, each of which is approximately 125 kilometres away. Lorelei was the youngest of four children, two girls and two boys, and like Gareth, she had the privilege of being raised in a Christian home.

Church, Sunday School and a Christian home combined to provide Lorelei with a sound background in the gospel truth. Although always aware of her need to become a Christian it was not until she was eleven years old that she was really challenged to make that vital decision and take the important step of receiving Jesus Christ. Her Sunday School teacher led her to faith in the Saviour.

Lorelei enjoyed the fellowship and company of other young Christians at school and church through her teenage years. Her family was also a great source of strength and support through that time. In 1990 Lorelei felt the call of God at a church camp and surrendered her life to full time service. She then entered The Fundamental Bible College for Asians in Tarlac. During those formative years Dr. Myron Guiler was a regular visitor to the Philippines. Dr. Guiler was the president of the mission board Independent Baptist Mission for Asians which is closely associated with the college in Tarlac where Lorelei was enrolled.

At the end of her three-year course Lorelei was considering her future and God's purpose for her life. It was then she received an offer of a scholarship to enroll for a four-year course at the Marietta Bible College. The College has a programme in which they train a number of foreign students in order to equip them to return to their respective countries and engage in church planting and other ministries. The Marietta Bible College charges no tuition fees to these foreign students.

Although she was reluctant to leave home and family Lorelei stepped out in faith and left in March 1993. Like other students in Marietta, Lorelei was given opportunity for involvement in the ministries of the Marietta Bible Center Church. These included Sunday School, Bus Ministry, Nursery, Christian Camps, Visitation Programme, Choir and Children's Church.

She was well settled at the Bible School and beginning her third year when Gareth McDowell arrived to begin his studies. Lorelei remembered what it had been like for her as a new comer and was among those who tried to help Gareth settle in to college life. Little did Lorelei know that this new comer would some day be her husband.

In January 1997 Gareth travelled with Lorelei to the Philippines to ask Mr. Cunanan for Lorelei's hand in marriage. It was readily given, and the happy couple planned for a wedding later that year.

Included in their future plans was the question about where they might work. As best they knew how, they surrendered their lives to God for His will. While visiting with Lorelei's family in Tarlac, Gareth was able to travel with his wife-to-be to various parts of the Philippines' main island where he found that Roman Catholicism was still the predominant religion. Running parallel with Catholicism there were widespread superstitions, occult and voodoo practices among the general population. The southern Island of Mindanao is a stronghold for Islam where some militant elements have been aligned with Ossama bin Laden's terrorist groups.

Both Gareth and Lorelei were struck by the great need, the openness of the people and their hunger for the Word of God. Gareth was also dismayed to discover that there was not sufficient Bible literature to meet the great demand and opportunity. This was the first indication to Gareth and Lorelei of what God might have for them in their future ministry.

It was a beautiful but hot day on the 15 August 1997 when Gareth and Lorelei were married at the Marietta Bible Center Church in Ohio. Family and friends from Northern Ireland and the Philippines joined with fellow students to witness the happy couple exchange vows before God as Dr. Myron Guiler conducted the wedding ceremony.

After Lorelei graduated she taught at the Marietta Christian School while Gareth continued his studies at the college. During the college years the couple were able to make several visits to the Philippines, but they were still not sure where they should serve the Lord. Were they to settle in the United States, or would God have them return to Northern Ireland? Gareth could not forget the need, hunger and opportunity he had witnessed in the Philippines. The young couple earnestly prayed that God would confirm the right way ahead.

Corresponding with their pursuit to know and do God's will they received news from Every Home Crusade news sheet that workers were needed to distribute literature in the Philippines. Surely this is the right step? Gareth mused. After speaking with Ernie Allen and Samuel Adams of Every Home Crusade, Gareth and Lorelei decided that was the path they would follow.

After several months in the United States they returned to Northern Ireland to try to gather some funds for their work. At first Gareth thought of returning to his secular employment as an electrician to raise enough money to help them get started in the Philippines. However, this was not to be God's way for Gareth and Lorelei. They felt challenged to step out in faith without the backing of a mission board or any guaranteed support.

In November 2000 the young couple left for the Philippines where they took up residence with Lorelei's family in Tarlac. Within a few weeks the first supply of Every Home Crusade literature arrived: four boxes containing the booklets, Light of the World, The Way of Salvation and the Gospel of John. After the first consignment of literature was exhausted Gareth received another thirty boxes from Every Home Crusade. The quantity shipped from Belfast to the Philippines continued to grow until a container full of literature was needed to help satisfy the great need.

Using the contacts provided through Lorelei's brother, Pastor Ferdinand Cunanan, Gareth was able to build up a strategic distribution network, which widened out from Tarlac to a radius of more than 300 miles. Within a short time 300 pastors were being supplied with gospel material for evangelistic use in their areas. Some would travel more than eight hours to pick up their quota of evangelistic material.

Utilising the training they received at the Marietta Bible College, Gareth and Lorelei set up seminars where they train workers in churches and then help them conduct evangelistic literature programmes in their local churches. This has opened doors for them to go on evangelistic treks with Filipino Christians. These open doors have brought greater demand for more literature, and Every Home Crusade has been sending increased quotas to the McDowells to help satisfy the need.

Although Gareth receives literature from some other publishing houses, individuals and other organisations, he confesses that without Every Home Crusade their work would not be possible. Teams from Northern Ireland and elsewhere have visited Gareth and Lorelei and have been able to engage in the literature distribution programme.

For almost ten years Every Home Crusade has been sending large quantities of their literature to Mr. James Tioco, a prosperous businessman in Manila. He uses his company's warehouses to unload the containers and store the large quantities of literature. The same firm's transport network transfers the precious literature to Christian workers all over the Philippines. In recent years James has also been working closely with Gareth and Lorelei to supply their area.

Gareth's close involvement with so many pastors opened up another ministry that he had never anticipated. While visiting many of these pastors in their homes and churches he noticed that they had very few theological resources. For some years Gareth's Dad, Errol McDowell, had indulged in a worthwhile hobby. He collected, bought and sold second hand theological books. It was more than just a coincidence that Errol's hobby matched the need for more adequate theological resources for the Filipino pastors.

Book Aid, a Christian ministry dedicated to providing books for pastors in the Third World, was glad to supply Gareth with material for needy pastors in the Philippines. This ministry has been most effective in equipping many Christian workers who hitherto had been bereft of any good devotional and sound theological books.

As a result of Gareth and Lorelei sending literature, booklets and books to these Christian workers, numerous letters return assuring them of how God is using the material.

Here are some of the requests, letters and reports which have been received:

OPEN DOOR BAPTIST CHURCH
Zaragosa, Nueva Ecija
Pastor Don Roda
We still continue the work by giving gospel tracts and soul winning. It's a challenging work; lots of struggles, some are rejecting us, throwing the tracts away or tearing them up, but praise God for He's always working in the hearts of the sinners. Last month we had eight souls who got saved.
We thank you for your prayers and support. We thank you for the Bibles and gospel tracts that you extended to us. Thank you for the encouragement that you're giving us. We cannot repay you but we know, God can. Please remember us always in your prayers to achieve our goals for the glory of God.

••••

OPEN DOOR BAPTIST MISSION
Sta. Maria, Pangasinan
Pastor Francis S. Teodoro Jr.
On behalf of my church, we would like to express our gratitude for having you deeply involved with many churches. You became a blessing to us by giving Bibles and gospel tracts and I thank God very much.
The Lord blessed us again by adding souls and more Bible studies open.

••••

KAPATIRANG CRISTIANO CHURCH
San Miguel, Tarlac
Pastor Dandy Frias
We distributed all the tracts we got from you and we still need more. It is interesting that people are gladly receiving the tracts. We are distributing in city parks, bus terminals and house to house.

Sir, please, if you could give us more Bibles and Tagalog tracts, we shall appreciate it so much.

••••

MAJESTY INDEPENDENT BAPTIST MISSION
Olongapo City
Pastor Nino Ian S. Bumanlag
In its fledgling existence as a mission, I found it very difficult to reach out to people without some material aids to use like tracts, Bibles and Sunday School materials. I was informed that there is a couple who willingly share these things for the ministry.   Please share us some.

••••

FUNDAMENTAL INDEPENDENT BAPTIST CHURCH
UNGOT, Tarlac City
We would like to request for any materials available which we can use for our ministries and give to our members to help them grow in their faith. I am also planning to give materials to the three Public Elementary Schools which are in our area to reach them for the Lord.
We appreciate every materials that you can give and promise to distribute them for free and use them for the work of the Lord.

••••

LIBERTY BIBLE BAPTIST CHURCH
Bagulin, La Union
Pastor Elizar Ponciano
Our Church is in need of Tracts, Bibles, Posters and Sunday School materials.  We are requesting for your support of these materials in order for us to reach thousands of lost souls and share the gospel.

••••

MISSION WORK
Bustos, Bulacan
Pastor Winiefred L. Antazo
We are now in great need of gospel tracts, Bibles or any literature that would give us an advantage in the ministry. For this reason, may we request your good office for any evangelism materials that we could use in the ministry.

••••

CALVARY BAPTIST CHURCH
Vigan City
Pastor Melvin B. Armandico
I have heard of your ministry in helping churches with materials like Bibles, tracts, posters, Sunday School lessons, etc. I was very much encouraged because ministries like yours go on in our nation.
Your generosity will always be remembered and forever be appreciated. God Bless You!

••••

BIBLE FAITH BELIEVERS BAPTIST CHURCH
Mexico, Pampanga
Pastor Mario R. Son
Brother, it will be a great help for our fellow pastors who did not receive yet, to give them Bibles and Tracts for their ministries. May God Bless you and your ministry.

••••

Gareth and Lorelei continue to work closely with Every Home Crusade but they stand in urgent need of suitable premises to accommodate this growing ministry in this strategic region.

Gareth and Lorelei summed up the impact of Every Home Crusade's contribution to their ministry in their report sent for *Good*

*News*, the monthly newsletter from Every Home Crusade Newsletter, in February 2005.

> We received about five hundred boxes of literature from Sowers of the Word Ministries last May. Everything arrived in excellent condition, and we were sure glad to see the large amount of gospel literature that you sent us. Thank you very, very much. A year ago you asked me how long it would take to distribute a container of Literature. I told you about six months. I was not sure at that time if it was at all possible, but praise the Lord we have a God who makes all things possible. All was gone not in six months but in two months only. Two weeks later the house where the literature had been stored was flooded due to a typhoon.
>
> All the gospel literature was distributed to more than two hundred pastors and many more were requesting for supplies. The literature was given to people in the three main islands (Luzon, Visayas and Mindanao). The gospel tracts were used in open air meetings, buses, schools, hospitals, and in the markets. The Sunday School Bible Lessons are in everyday use in the children's meetings. All of the literature has become instrumental in the salvation of many and in the starting of Bible studies around the churches.
>
> Many Pastors send their sincere thanks for the blessing you have been to their people. My wife and I thank you again for allowing us to be part of your ministry. We are looking forward to receiving a further 100,000 scripture booklets, 1,000 sets of Bible lessons and a very large quantity of gospel tracts.

Gareth and Lorelei McDowell.

# 10

## THE HEART OF AFRICA
## TOUCHES MAIZIE SMYTH'S HEART

Singing has always been a major feature of the great revivals around the world. It was no different in the heart of Africa when a great spiritual awakening visited the Belgian Congo in 1954. First, came brokenness and repentance among the Christians, foreign missionaries and national pastors alike. Tens of thousands of people were converted and churches were packed. The initial tears and brokenness gave way to songs of joy, praise and thanksgiving.

These African believers would need their songs to help them through the next fifty years of brutal persecution and bloody revolution. The calamitous Zimba uprising of 1964 resulted in several dozens of foreign missionaries being martyred and thousands of Congolese Christians being slain. A virtual holocaust took place when the recurring political revolutions of this last decade were accompanied by the massacre of more than four million men, women and children. Tens of thousands of the surviving population had to flee from their homes and take refuge in the bush. Many who were scattered were separated from their families never to meet up with their loved ones again.

Through all the dark days of these violent atrocities most people lost almost all they possessed, even though they originally never had very much. However, Christians never lost their song. The cruel uprisings had left whole congregations bereft of Bibles, New Testaments and nearly all their Christian literature. They survived the fiery trial of their faith by hiding God's Word in their hearts and recalling the hymns they had learned to sing. They had no hymnbooks.

Maizie Smyth, a missionary with UFM Worldwide, lived in the heart of this troubled part of Africa for more than twenty years until she had to be evacuated from the region for her own safety. Living in her native Northern Ireland Maizie continued to supply the African believers in the Kisangani, Banalia, Bafwasende and Bumba districts with most of the supplies they needed to maintain the Mission clinics.

Some of her Christian friends appealed to her in letters making all sorts of unusual requests. On one occasion Maizie received an appeal from Christians in Kisangani. A pastor wrote, "I have no shirt for Sunday church. . . could you please buy me one?" Another sent a piece of paper on which he had obviously outlined the size and shape of his children's feet and asked if Maizie could go to a second-hand market to buy shoes for his children.

One particular letter surprised Maizie as it neither asked for personal items nor for medicines nor surgical equipment. Instead, the church leaders collectively asked Maizie to help them acquire seventy thousand new hymnbooks for the two thousand Mission churches in the Congo. The old hymnbooks which had survived the tumultuous years were tattered, torn and falling apart. To reprint in the Congo was so prohibitive that the ordinary church people could never afford them. Furthermore, the old church hymnals had been published separately in two different languages, Lingala and Swahili, and this created difficulties in some areas where not everyone spoke both languages.

As resourceful and undaunted as ever, Maizie took the request to Mr. Ernie Allen and his friends at Every Home Crusade in Belfast. It was a mammoth project, but the team at EHC did not hesitate to accept the challenge of publishing a new hymnbook for the Congo as long as Maizie would compile it, including hymns in French, Lingala and Swahili.

Maizie applied herself to the job. When she had finished her part, the presses began to roll at the Every Home Crusade factory. It was a great day when seventy thousand new hymnbooks rolled off the press, were stacked into boxes in Belfast and soon were on their way to Kisangani, Congo.

This major operation was a great encouragement to the Congolese believers who were ecstatic about their new books. It also helped cement a bond between them and believers outside the Congo, assuring them that other Christians in Ireland who knew their friend Maizie, also cared for them.

Maizie Smyth was born and raised on the lower slopes of County Antrim's Slemish Mountain where young Saint Patrick, Ireland's Patron Saint, tended his sheep and viewed his native Scotland. In the townland of Greenhill, just over four miles outside the beautiful village of Broughshane, Maizie with her brother and sister, spent the long summer days playing or working in the surrounding hay fields of the family home and farm. Although, it was not all play and Maizie was never a stranger to work. Besides rounding up sheep and lambs she was a regular cowhand and also gave a hand to work on the crops long before the days of noisy combine harvesters.

Cross Primary School also played a big part in Maizie's early life, where apart from learning the basic elements of education her teacher, Miss Thompson, faithfully taught her pupils God's Word. Every day Maizie heard how much God loves sinners. Miss Thompson began every morning by teaching the Scriptures and never missed an opportunity to teach about the Lord Jesus Christ.

After seven years at the small rural school, young Maizie moved to the large secondary school in Ballymena. Whatever the weather, she and her brother and sister had to cycle to the Battery bus stop where they ditched their bicycles before catching the bus for the eight-mile journey to Ballymena.

Life in high school was very different. Miss Thompson was not there to teach the Word of God. However, during the course of Maizie's first year at secondary school, several Faith Mission Pilgrims came to have a tent mission near her home at Greenhill. After most of the farm chores were finished one Sunday evening Maizie decided to go to the small evangelistic tent. The lady preacher spoke from John's Gospel where Jesus said, "I am the door; by me if any man enter in, he shall be saved."

Twelve-year-old Maizie listened intently to the preacher and knew that God was speaking to her. She was in turmoil. Although she knew she needed to be saved, she tried to postpone the matter and argued with herself as to whether or not she should become a Christian that night. The battle raged within her heart until fear finally won, and she decided against taking that important step.

Her heart continued to be troubled on the way home that summer evening. Even though it was late the hens still needed to be rounded up. Just when she thought they were all safely gathered into their houses and was about to close up, she discovered one hen still running around the field.

Maizie tried for more than ten minutes to steer that stray hen to the safety of the hen house. It suddenly struck her that it was a vivid reflection of her own life. She was the straying and rebellious sinner and even though God had set before her an open door of salvation through Christ yet she persisted in running in the opposite direction. As soon as she was able to coax the hen into the hen house she wasted no time to go to her room, and at her bedside Maizie asked the Lord Jesus to be her Saviour.

After four years at secondary school Maizie enrolled at Ballymena Technical College for a two year shorthand and typing course. Once she acquired her certificate she got a job with a dairy firm in Ballymena, but she had a longing to work in Belfast where her sister Isobel already worked. She was delighted to get an office job with the Down County Education Committee, and Maizie boarded at the Presbyterian Hostel in the city where Isobel lived.

During her time at the Presbyterian Hostel Maizie met many Christian young people who were very keen for the Lord and were not ashamed to openly confess their faith in Jesus Christ. Maizie not only envied them, she decided to join them in attending the Christian Endeavour at Berry Street Presbyterian Church.

It was there that Maizie had a spiritual wake up call. One evening Nancy Bell, one of the leaders, approached Maizie and inquired, "You're a Christian, aren't you?" When Maizie answered positively Nancy asked, "Will you please open the meeting in prayer." Maizie panicked. The only prayer Maizie could think of was Joseph Scriven's well-known hymn, "What a Friend we Have in Jesus". That simple prayer was Maizie's first step into her involvement with the Berry Street Christian Endeavour.

Rev. Joe Wright, a former missionary to Brazil and the Irish secretary for Unevangelized Fields Mission, had his office just a few doors away from the Presbyterian Hostel. Joe was a very enthusiastic person, and although he was looked upon as a veteran missionary he had a lot of time for young people.

At the hostel Joe introduced the young people to a monthly prayer meeting for the UFM missionaries all over the world. Maizie and her newly acquired Christian friends who lived at the hostel decided to attend the meeting. Through that prayer meeting Maizie learned to pray more spontaneously, and periodically she had opportunity to meet various visiting missionaries.

Not only did Maizie learn to pray through that meeting, but she also discovered that the more she prayed for the missionaries the more God challenged her to do something to help them. Soon she found out first hand that there was a great joy in giving to God's work also, but she never thought God would want more than that.

A visit by Fred Rainey of Child Evangelism Fellowship to Berry Street Christian Endeavour in October 1966 made an indelible impression upon Maizie's life. The nation was in mourning following the terrible disaster at Aberfan in the Welsh valleys when a slag heap gave way and engulfed a primary school in the town. Over one hundred and forty children lost their lives. Understandably there was a sombre mood in the meeting, and Fred closed his address with a challenge, "If Aberfan had happened on your street, how many boys and girls would be in heaven today because you had led them to Christ?"

At the end of that meeting Maizie was so challenged that she decided to ask Fred if there was any possibility of helping to teach God's Word to the boys and girls in South Belfast. Within a few weeks Fred made it possible for Maizie to start teaching in the children's meetings at McClure Street City Mission Hall.

Maizie's social and Christian life was developing very satisfactorily with the security of a good job and the opportunity to serve the Lord amongst the boys and girls in South Belfast. She never dreamed that God could be asking more of her. But He did. Just when she had thought of upgrading her car to a new Mini, God spoke to her during a meeting in Great Northern Street City Mission Hall. She had taken friends from work in the hope and earnest prayer that God would speak to them. It was Maizie that God spoke to through the preacher's text in Luke 12:15, "Take heed, and beware of covetousness: for a man's life consisteth not in the abundance of the things which he possesseth."

At first Maizie tried to dismiss any thought from her mind that God would be speaking to her. She was not a covetous person. On the following Sunday she was dumbfounded when God spoke to her again at her home church when the Reverend Porter preached from the same text. However, she reasoned that God could not be specifically speaking to her about going to Bible School.

Maizie reasoned that if God really wanted her in Bible School then He would have to either put her out of her job or put her out of the house she shared with two friends in South Belfast. Just when she thought that either one of these propositions was impossible, God spoke again. Over an early morning cup of tea one of her fellow boarders spoke up, "Maizie, things have changed a little here. The elderly owner of this house believes it is time for her to sell and move nearer to her son in England. She has given us one month to look for another house."

Maizie was dumbfounded. God had spoken so unmistakably. Being a Ballymena woman she was always keen to bargain, but she found she could not bargain with God. He was asking for full surrender to His will. Maizie yielded her all the Lord Jesus and soon entered the Bible Training Institute in Glasgow to prepare for Christian service.

••••

Maizie was invited to a UFM Missionary Weekend at Netherhall in Largs, Scotland, by Bill Gilvear, a former Missionary to Zaire. It was during that weekend she discovered the next step in her amazing journey that would take her to the heart of Africa. Although Maizie had set her mind on going to the south of Ireland with CEF it seemed that during that weekend she was bombarded with more and more information and challenged about Africa.

She listened to reports of how Christians and missionaries had survived terrible days of brutal persecution and felt there was no way she could go to a place like that. Furthermore, missionaries in the Belgian Congo, now renamed Zaire, spoke Swahili, French and Lingala. Maizie felt it was impractical that a Broughshane girl like herself could ever rise to such a challenge. She was sure God would never ask her. But He did.

In spite of her reticence and sense of inadequacy God persisted in speaking to Maizie. She related:

As if the Lord heard my protest Psalm 32:8 kept repeating in my head; "I will instruct thee and teach thee in the way which thou shalt go; I will guide thee with mine eye." For over a week there was a daily struggle about Zaire. I told the Lord that I was only a secretary, and what He needed in Zaire were linguists, doctors, nurses or teachers. There was no way He would want me there.

At BTI on Friday mornings we had the missions lecture and frequently a missionary came to that class and spoke of their work. On the Friday following the conference I was still agitated about what I had heard at the meetings and what I should do. I was shocked when I discovered that the speaker at the missions' lecture was a missionary from Zaire although he worked with another mission. To be truthful, I found his talk quite boring, but his finishing statement hit home, "You may not be a doctor, nurse or teacher, but you can communicate the gospel. In Zaire today God needs people who know they are called by Him and those who can reach out to all levels of the community."
I was dumbfounded.

While other students went to their next lecture Maizie made a hasty retreat to her room where she wept uncontrollably before God and through those tears she surrendered again to the will of God.

Following the process of applying to the UFM, completing the candidates' course and being accepted by the Mission Council, Maizie attended an eight-month language course at a school in the French Alps. During those days she grappled with phonetics, the past, present and future tenses of regular and irregular verbs and other aspects of French grammar. Near to the end of the course a letter from Zaire informed her that the mission had decided to withdraw from the Zairian field.

Notwithstanding this major obstacle, Maizie was sure God had not brought her this far to lead her to a dead end. She and the other candidates persisted in prayer. It was a great day when news came through that missionaries would be admitted again to Zaire, and Maizie was assigned to the Theological College at Bunia and the Joint Mission Hospital at Nyankunde in North East Zaire under the umbrella of the Africa Inland Mission

••••

*Sifu* is what many of the children in Zaire appropriately called Maizie. Sifu is the Swahili word for praise, and Maizie was not only full of praise, but she had much to praise God for. Since she first arrived in Bunia in October, 1978 to this very day Maizie has so many chapters of her life for which she praises God.

Bunia was the commercial centre for Zaire's Ituri region. Many Greeks and Indians had opened shops in the town, and their businesses helped bring a lot of needed finance and development to the city. However, one of the big disadvantages was the lack of communication by telephone. This meant Maizie had to adjust to long silences and learn much patience.

Maizie taught the Child Evangelism course at the theological school, and after two years there she was appointed director of the Woman's Bible School. This presented many opportunities and challenges. Not only was she preparing effective missionaries for the Ituri region, she saw many of her students become suitable helpmeets for the pastors who were graduating from the Theological College.

After ten happy and fruitful years in Bunia Maizie had longings to go to Kisangani, seven hundred kilometres away, the original area allocated by Evangelical Missions to UFM. This was the region that had experienced tremendous revival more than twenty years earlier, but it had been off limits to UFM missionaries because of division in the national leadership of the church. Consequently, the UFM field council felt that they could not provide missionary support to either side of a divided church, so their missionaries were withdrawn from the region. During her time in Bunia Maizie and her UFM colleagues never ceased praying that the Lord would bring about a reconciliation of the two factions, thus enabling the church and UFM to work together again.

In 1988 God answered that prayer. The Lord worked in hearts, and a very public and tearful reconciliation took place between the two discordant camps in the Kisangani churches. God did far above their expectations and the love between the believers was stronger than what it had been before the damaging rift.

During this reconciliation the Lord independently was urging Maizie to move to the Kisangani area. Maizie was due to travel to Northern Ireland for another furlough, but deep in her heart she knew that she probably would not return to work in Bunia.

During that year at home Maizie struggled with what the future held. Four months before returning to Zaire the UFM Council in London wrote to her, "There are no arrangements yet for Kisangani therefore you need to return to the work in Bunia." Although Maizie accepted the Mission's directive, she was still not satisfied that this was God's way for her.

The next evening Maizie met with some of her colleagues who had worked in Kisangani in earlier years. She chatted with them about the situation in Kisangani and what she was planning to do when she returned to Zaire. She shared with them her dilemma, "I thought in my heart that God was opening the way for me to go to Kisangani. Now the Mission Council have told me that until a green light is given by the churches the Mission is advising me to plan on returning to Bunia."

Maizie was shocked when her colleagues disclosed that they also thought God was calling them back to Kisangani. For the rest of the night they discussed, reasoned, planned and prayed about returning to Kisangani. Maize was so excited she sang God's praises and prayed all the way home to Broughshane. She went to bed, but there was no sleep. Her mind was overactive and her heart overjoyed.

On arrival in Zaire Maizie attended meetings with her colleagues from the UFM International Sending Council. They listened to Maizie's plans and helped her put together a future strategy for the ministry in Kisangani. Although there were some set backs and not all those who had planned to go back to Kisangani were able to fulfill their proposals, Maizie and her colleague Carol persisted with their plans.

The Kisangani climate was much hotter than in Bunia and the humidity was almost unbearable at times. Furthermore, Kisangani did not have a hospital with adequate facilities. Any complicated or lengthy medical emergencies would have to be referred to the out of the way Mission Hospital in Nyankunde. However, nothing could deter Maizie and Carol fulfilling what they felt God had put in their hearts.

Maizie had to pack up ten years of living in Bunia into one large container. With the God-sent help of some German missionary friends the container was transported down the bumpy road to Kisangani.

The first days in Kisangani were spent greeting hundreds of people who came to visit the missionaries. The locals had to share their experiences of all that had happened during the ten years since the missionaries left.

Kisangani is the capital of the Upper Zaire region and the hub for government administration for that area. The headquarters of the organisation responsible for the evangelical Protestant churches in Northeast Zaire was also located in Kisangani. This meant that a lot of conferences for the leaders from the various churches were held locally and many of these leaders were former students from Bunia who had been trained at Maizie's "kitchen sink" at the college. Frequently they stayed in Maizie's home.

Maizie was overwhelmed with the opportunities for ministry in Kisangani and in the surrounding areas. The sheer magnitude of the task convinced her that the only way ahead was to train young people to do the work of the ministry. First of all she had to help them financially and practically to obtain a basic education and then go on to college and seminary.

Bunia was far away for some of these students and financially prohibitive so the Lord enabled Maizie to help in the French Bible Institute at Banjwade, a village sixty-four kilometres from Kisangani. As well as working in the Bible Institute in Banjwade, Maizie helped by providing regular medical supplies for use in the clinics there. Maizie spent two nights every week at Banjwade, and the balance of her time was spent working with the church leaders in Kisangani. Beyond these responsibilities Maizie also conducted seminars in remote villages in the bush and in some of the small settlements dotted along the River Congo.

Door after door began to open for Maizie in towns and villages that had been closed since the rebellion of 1964. At times she felt that the demanding schedule was more than she could cope with. However, God gave her joy and strength beyond her human energies.

In 1996 the Lord opened the door for Samuel Adams of Every Home Crusade to visit East and Central Africa with UFM missionary Eric Magowan, one of Maizie's colleagues who had spent many years in that region. Samuel published a report of his trip in the Every Home Crusade newsletter.

> Two friends gave me a very generous gift to enable me to visit Kenya and Zaire. As a result of this I was able to visit Nairobi, Kenya for ten days and spend another ten days in Zaire. I was very pleased to be accompanied with Mr. Eric Magowan who has been a missionary in Zaire and in Nairobi. This visit allowed me to see at first hand the importance of the literature which we have been sending to many friends, and also to see the tremendous need for the scripture booklets, gospel tracts and leaflets.
>
> The city of Nairobi with a population of 2,000,000 people is a city of contrasts - there are large office blocks and beautiful homes where wealthy people live while the majority live in terrible poverty.
>
> My first day was spent in the Soweto Slum, where Eric has been working with a small church. As we walked with the local Christians through the slum, and viewed the wooden and tin shacks which are home to thousands of people, we could see, and smell the results of no running water or sewage system in this district where these people live.
>
> Far worse is the spiritual condition in which these people are living under the powers of darkness, without knowing the love of our Lord Jesus Christ in their lives. However, it was encouraging to see both young and old alike keen to receive copies of the Scripture booklet *The Way of Salvation Through Our Lord Jesus Christ* in a variety of languages.
>
> As a result of the evangelistic outreach of this small church in Soweto, many souls have been saved, and these new Christians are slowly leaving this slum area and returning to

their home villages. Carrying their faith with them these young converts are now opening small churches in these villages.

In Zaire we visited the headquarters of 'Diguna' which is a German Mission. They have large lorries which are designed for the extremely bad road conditions within Zaire. Teams of young German Christians drive these lorries for hundreds of miles in Zaire, until they arrive in the region which they wish to evangelise. They then collect the local pastors and evangelists and take them to preach the gospel in the villages within their own area.

The Diguna Team provides loud-speaking equipment, and has supplies of our literature for distribution to the people who attend the meetings.

I was very impressed with the vision and dedication of these teams of young Christians. During my visit a total of nine teams were in different parts of Zaire, with at least one team being "on the road" for over three months.

Scripture booklets and gospel tracts are considered to be very valuable and are distributed with extreme care due to their scarcity. Each pastor may be given only thirty scripture booklets for distribution in a day during which they will conduct seven open-air meetings.

Kurt Zander is one of the leaders of Diguna Mission in Zaire. As I discussed with him the literature needs of Diguna workers, we realised that we need to send them a full container load of tracts, leaflets and booklets.

We were very pleased to visit Miss Maizie Smyth in Kisangani, Zaire. Conditions in Zaire are very difficult with extreme poverty everywhere. Most people can only afford one meagre meal per day.

As we stayed with Maizie we noticed that there was a constant stream of people visiting her - pastors, evangelists, young and old, all wanting to share with her their own particular problems.

Maizie showed real compassion, love and concern as she patiently listened, counselled and helped these people.

We visited a Bible School where every home and classroom is built with sticks, mud and grass. These students have only a handful of study books. They have felt the call of God upon their lives, and want to study to become pastors to their own people.

After travelling forty miles on dirt roads Maizie teaches two days a week in the Banjwade Bible School. It is thrilling to see the spirituality and humility in the lives of these students. One of the students whom we met had been a local government official. When he got saved he had thirteen wives. For a time he prayed about this situation one by one these wives left him, and now he is in Bible School with one wife.

On Sunday we attended church and were thrilled to see a full church with 500-600 in attendance. Sadly we noticed there were hardly any hymn books available for the people in the church services. This is a common problem in most of the churches.

Maizie told us that in some of the village churches, if the pastor is away for any reason, they simply cancel the church service, as no one else has got a copy of the Bible. As I discussed the needs for literature with the leaders of the evangelism department, I asked, "How long will it take to distribute the literature which you have at present?"

He replied "We could distribute it all in one day, as the people are so eager to receive it. But we are very careful how we distribute the booklets and tracts as we do not know how long it will be until we receive another supply of literature."

Maizie was working with a the Bible School teacher to translate more tracts, and the booklet Pardon and Assurance, into the Lingala language. We hope to print these and send another container of literature to Maizie in Kisangani.

In Nairobi I visited various Mission and Denomination Headquarters which have a total of about 7,000 churches in their care across Kenya. I heard the same message time after time - "We have no tracts or anything like these Scripture booklets." – "We don't have tracts, they are far too expensive." "Pastors constantly come to us for supplies of tracts, but we don't have any to give to them".

When I explained that we would be willing to send to them large supplies of our tracts, leaflets and booklets completely free of charge, they always answered in the same excited manner, "We wish we had known about your literature ministry years ago. You have brought great joy to our hearts today. Please send immediately 300,000 Scripture booklets in English, Swahili, Kamba, Kikuyu and Luo."

Mr. Ed Morrow gave us lists of requests which had been received from many pastors and evangelists who had come to him for supplies of tracts.

We attended an open-air meeting in the centre of Nairobi, when hundreds of people including the street children stopped and listened to the gospel message being preached. At the end of the meeting a very short appeal was made and about twenty people came forward professing to accept Jesus Christ to be their Saviour.

Scripture booklets were then distributed. Four men were distributing bundles of Scripture booklets, but they couldn't move as people simply surrounded them, reaching out with empty hands, all trying to obtain a booklet before the supply was exhausted. Not one booklet was dropped on the ground.

On my last Sunday morning I quickly visited about five churches in Nairobi, in order to see as much as I could in the limited time. I was thrilled to see large churches - seating over 1,000 people - full, and with people sitting outside. Some of these churches have three services starting early on Sunday morning.

Even with churches full, the streets were crammed with people, still to be reached with the gospel message.
Also many false sects were having open air meetings of their own. As I looked at the masses of people in Kenya and Zaire I realised these people must be reached with the gospel message urgently, so that they may receive, "The Gift of God which is eternal life through Jesus Christ our Lord". This is why we are going to send a further container (19 Tonnes) of tracts, leaflets and booklets, to Kenya as soon as possible.

Samuel's visit to Africa stimulated greater vision and enthusiasm for the role literature was playing in the great work of evangelism in that continent. He tried to impart that same vision and enthusiasm to the workers at the EHC factory on his return from Africa.

••••

It was in 1992 that political unrest and hostility returned to the Northeast region of Zaire, and Maizie had to be evacuated from Kisangani to Kenya and then on home to Northern Ireland. She returned to Kisangani after three months at home in Broughshane, but the political tensions in Zaire continued to increase. This was followed by gunfire, plundering towns and looting shops. Some people were killed. At one stage some rebels threatened to take Maizie's Land Rover but the Lord protected Maizie and her vehicle.

Ferocious fighting came to Kisangani in 1997 when President Mobutu was ousted from the position he held for more than thirty years, and General Kabila introduced a new regime. During Mobutu's reign the country was known as Zaire but reverted to the Democratic Republic of Congo under President Kabila. Maizie just arrived back from furlough in time to witness the army of the new regime on the streets of Kisangani. Undaunted by their presence Maizie seized the opportunity to evangelise these young recruits. An effective way of doing this was to use the Every Home Crusade literature which had been sent from Belfast in large recycled tea chests. Throughout Maizie's time in Africa obtaining Bibles was always a problem. Availability was limited, and when they did arrive the price of a Bible was prohibitive for the local people.

Although an initial peace returned to the Congo after President Kabila assumed power, it was short lived. Days of uncertainty returned. Maizie was alone in Kisangani and had to maintain constant radio contact with various missionaries some 500 miles away to find news of what was happening. All of the missionaries were evacuated from the Bunia/Nyankunde areas, and this left Maizie feeling very alone and vulnerable. God comforted and protected her through that time.

Tensions continued to rise in Kisangani, and it soon became evident that there was going to be a confrontation of opposing armies in or near the town. Government soldiers marched through the town in a daily display of strength for the benefit of the local population. In spite of the impending threats, Maizie continued teaching her various classes. Rumours continued to circulate that the rebels were closing in on Kisangani.

One Saturday evening it all happened very suddenly. Maizie was sitting outdoors enjoying the cool of the evening with her neighbours. Suddenly, there was a loud burst of gunfire from the direction of the army camp followed by a continuous exchange of shooting which confirmed their worst fears that the rebels had arrived.

Maizie watched as hundreds of soldiers ran up and down the road using their automatic weapons to shoot into the air and frighten the local residents. The sporadic shooting continued for three days, but through it all God's peace filled Maizie's heart and her Congolese colleagues were a great encouragement.

In a miraculous way God preserved Maizie through six weeks of that threatening situation until she was finally evacuated for the second time out of Kisangani. As the plane lifted off from Congo on her way to Entebbe, Uganda, tears ran down her face. She looked below at Kisangani and the surrounding forest and prayed for so many of her friends who remained in this uncertain arena of conflict.

Maizie was very distressed as a result of having to leave the Congo in such a hurry. There had not even been time to say good bye to her friends. Those she had spoken to asked her not to forget their plight. Although Maizie knew it was necessary to leave, the Congo would very much remain on her heart. Maizie did not know it then, but this was not the end of her ministry to the land she loved. It was only the beginning of a new chapter that would become a more fruitful ministry with far-reaching effects on Africa.

Initially Maizie contemplated going to another UFM field but only seemed to come up against many brick walls. She had no peace or enthusiasm to think of serving the Lord elsewhere, but the news filtering through from the Congo continued to make it too dangerous to return. There had been an escalation of the conflict with Ugandan and Rwandan soldiers competing to take control of the region.

Appeals from Africa motivated Maizie to work on behalf of the Congolese church. Besides the lack of food, medical supplies had dried up and there were no funds to buy medicines. She travelled to Kampala in Uganda to meet with some church leaders to discuss how she could help. As a result Maizie committed herself to co-ordinate various relief programmes to which UFM council gave her their full backing.

Maizie could clearly see God's hand controlling and guiding her life and opening a door to be a back-up worker for her friends in Kisangani. She campaigned on behalf of the Congolese church, promoting prayer support and raising funds for food, medicines, Bibles and Christian literature. It was at this stage that Every Home Crusade rose to the challenge to provide seventy thousand hymn books in the French, Swahili and Lingala languages.

As well as supplying the hymnbooks Every Home Crusade had been supplying quantities of Bible literature in various languages for the church in the Congo for many years. It was while Maizie was based in Ireland for a prolonged period that she became more acquainted with the magnitude of the EHC work. She was staggered to learn that they produced Scriptures in over seventy languages and sent them to more than one hundred countries throughout the world.

When Maizie visited their factory in Belfast she was astonished to discover they were printing three tons of gospel literature every day.

Mr. Ernie Allen, founder of the Revival Movement and Every Home Crusade in Ireland, was a giant of the faith. His passion was for God, grace and the gospel. Mr. Allen had a dedicated team of more than twenty workers ably organised by Samuel Adams, all of whom were fully committed to sending out good quality Christian literature.

Maizie was taken aback one day when she received an invitation to pay a visit to the EHC office. At that meeting Ernie Allen and Samuel Adams explained that they had received numerous requests for literature from various African countries, most of which were English and French speaking. Although EHC endeavoured to honour all these orders, they were concerned that they had little knowledge of the recipients of this literature. They invited Maizie to help them by visiting some of these African countries to make contact with church leaders and make them aware of the ministry of Every Home Crusade.

The more Maizie thought and prayed about the invitation the more excited she became and felt she could engage in this work while still carrying on her relief programmes for the Congolese church. Furthermore, it would take Maize to some other African countries where UFM missionaries were already serving the Lord.

Maizie's first trip to West Africa took her to Cameroon, the Central African Republic and Ivory Coast and gave her a great insight to what was happening in other parts of Africa. In some places she was discouraged to see the slow growth of churches in comparison to what God was doing in the Congo. It also gave her a deeper appreciation for how the Congolese leaders had risen to the task and taken responsibility for the leadership and administration of their own churches for many years, whereas she discovered elsewhere in Africa there were still too many situations where the missionaries were still needed to run the show.

Other situations were very encouraging. In Ivory Coast she visited a missionary who had returned to Abidjan to set up a small printing press. Maizie set off early one morning to find Victor and his print shop. When she finally located his whereabouts she was made very welcome, but Victor was not available immediately. While she waited she felt that the loud noise of the printing presses and the folding machines was almost unbearable and wondered how the workers could tolerate the agitation. When she looked in on them more closely they seemed to be oblivious to the uproar. It was only after a few minutes Maizie realized they were totally unaware of the noise for they were deaf and only communicated with each other by sign language.

When she finally met Victor, Maizie mentioned that she noticed all his workers seemed to be deaf. He explained that was one of the reasons why he returned to Ivory Coast. He was burdened for this small group of deaf Christians who had no employment and felt God would have him set up the press and train the group in printing techniques. They were printing some books in French and publishing gospel leaflets for use across West Africa. The only person on the staff who could speak besides Victor was the receptionist.

From Gabon Maizie travelled to Cameroon. While she was there Maizie met with several Korean missionaries. Many years earlier the government in Gabon had invited Koreans to install a new communication system. More than eighty Koreans arrived to complete the job. After a month in Gabon the workers sent word back to Korea they needed a pastor. The government paid for a Korean pastor and family to come to Gabon and minister to the Koreans.

Not only did these workers form a Korean church, the pastor and his team also started a Bible School for the young Gabonese. That Bible School met a great need in the city and provided evangelists to reach other parts of Gabon with the gospel. When Maizie met with them and explained the work of Every Home Crusade they were so excited to hear that they could obtain the EHC literature for their outreach programme.

While in Yaounde she met up with a friend who had started a programme in Kinshasa for Pygmy evangelism. Maizie was glad their paths crossed again and was able to offer the help of EHC evangelistic literature. The Korean friends proved to be people of vision and energy for God's work. They were building a Bible Seminary and a new church in Yaounde and were elated when Maizie shared with them the vision of Every Home Crusade.

From Cameroon Maizie proceeded to the Central African Republic even though it was difficult to obtain a visa for this impoverished country. There she met with some workers from the Brethren Mission who showed great interest in the EHC literature.

During her last hours in Central African Republic she met a visiting missionary who had just arrived from the United States via Ivory Coast. As Maizie was checking out of the guesthouse to catch her next flight this visitor was checking in. The lady at the desk asked this new arrival what his business was. He explained that he was Director of Evangelism Explosion and asked the lady for directions to the Bible Society as he wanted to find copies of *The Gospel of John* for use in a coming evangelistic enterprise. At that the lady spoke up and said, "You need to look no further for that is why Maizie is here."

With only five minutes to spare Maizie was able to arrange to have a supply of *The Gospel of John* sent to Evangelism Explosion for use in their work. The visitor ordered a further twenty-four thousand copies of John's Gospel for Gabon with the assurance that other orders would follow.

••••

After Maizie returned from each trip to Africa she presented requests to Mr. Allen and Samuel Adams for millions of tracts and tens of thousands of gospel booklets. For weeks and months after her return Maizie received letters and e-mails from numerous contacts soliciting Every Home Crusade to help supply literature for their churches.

On a trip to Kampala in relation to her relief programme Maizie had to stop off in Nairobi for a day. The plane for Kampala was due to leave the next morning so she joined up with two African friends for coffee at a local café that afternoon in order to catch up on all their news. While they were enjoying their coffee and fellowship a man approached their table. He was an African so Maizie sat back to allow him to speak to her friends, but he pointed his finger at her and said, "I wish to speak with you."

Maizie had never seen this man before, but he produced one of her business cards from Every Home Crusade. When she asked where he got the card he explained that he was from Cameroon and had seen her picture when he returned home from a trip. This man pastored one of the principal churches in the area and was keen that EHC should supply them with literature.

So many orders for French literature arrived from Africa following her visits that the printing team at the EHC factory was glad of a break when Maizie reverted to making a few visits to the Congo. It allowed the team to fill requests from other parts of the world.

Samuel Adams then suggested Maizie should think of visiting Togo, Burkina Faso and Benin, all in the west of Africa. While on her way to speak at a ladies' meeting one evening in Belfast, Maizie was mulling over what Mr. Adams had proposed. She was not feeling very confident about making the trip and expressed these doubts to the Lord.

Maizie tells the story in her own words.

The meeting went very well, but during the closing hymn God spoke to my heart. I sang the familiar hymn like I never had sung it before, "Anywhere with Jesus I can safely go." I felt my reservations about the trip were legitimate. I was heading off into the unknown and to three countries where I did not know anyone; at least I didn't think I knew anyone. All uncertainty was swept away by the time we reached the end of that hymn and during the drive home that night I was already formulating plans for the trip to West Africa.

I arrived in Lome, the capital of Togo, late on the Saturday and made my way to prearranged accommodation in a self-catering guesthouse. Because I didn't have any local currency I had great difficulty persuading a nearby shop owner to sell me bread, milk and a few other basic essentials.

The following morning, Sunday, there was no one else in the guesthouse and the guard did not speak French so I did not know what to do or where to go. I did what I instinctively do in such predicaments, I prayed and asked the Lord to direct me for I was there to do His work. After that word of prayer I walked to the main road where I hailed a taxi and agreed a price with him to take me to the nearest Baptist church. The fare was only about £0.30 so I knew he was not making too big a killing out of me. In fact, he didn't know of any Baptist churches in Lome for he was a Muslim, so he took me to the Catholic chapel.

I tried to explain to him that this was not the right church so he called to a lady on the street to ask directions. I could hardly believe what I heard when she said she was going to the Baptist church. I was already late. Most Sunday morning services in Africa begin at 9.00 a.m. and it was now 9.15 a.m. However, the lady told me their service started at 8.00 a.m. We were even later than I thought.

At the Baptist church I was ushered all the way to the front row and took my place just as the church secretary was making the announcements. All guests were asked to stand and introduce themselves. This gave me a welcome opportunity to say who I was and why I was in Lome.

I hoped to speak to the pastor after the service and inquire if there was an Alliance of Evangelical churches in Lome and where I might find their offices. Even later than my arrival, a man arrived and took his seat next to me at the front of the church. During the offering the stranger spoke to me and asked who I was and why I was in Lome. During the interaction that followed I discovered that he was the man I was looking for, the secretary of the Alliance of Evangelical churches in Togo. Why do I ever doubt God when He is so faithful and unerring?

Following the service we stayed behind to talk for a while and he gave me many names and addresses of local people I should contact. Armed with the names and addresses I left early Monday to present the literature ministry of EHC to various Christian leaders. I soon discovered that the work regime in Togo is a little irregular.

The general population work from 8.00 a.m. until 12.00 noon and then rest until 3.00 p.m. after which they return to work until 5.30 or 6.00 p.m. It was most inconvenient to have to return five kilometres from the centre of town to the guesthouse at noon every day.

At Praise Chapel I met the church director who was most friendly and helpful. It was obvious he had a deep concern for reaching others with the gospel as he spoke of the work the church members and Bible School students were doing in the city. I thought he was somewhat discouraged in this work but when I mentioned this he told me the following story. A fellow arrived at their church who was curious to find out what went on there. After several visits he indicated he would like to become a follower of Jesus Christ whereupon the pastor led him to Christ. The new convert continued to attend all the meetings and in the prayer meetings he would pray for his family back home in his village on the Ghanaian border.

One day he approached the pastor and asked if the church would send someone to preach the gospel back in his village. The man said he was willing to help pay for a car to take them there. After some discussion and prayer the church finally decided to set up a visit to the man's home region. The pastor accompanied three church elders and discovered the village was in a very remote location.

They took a vehicle part of the way, but had to leave it and walk for miles before they reached this village. The new convert had already sent word ahead of the impending visit so the whole population was waiting to receive the delegation from Praise Chapel. Afterwards, the pastor confessed he had never seen such a sight. Village chiefs and all the people suspended their activities for four days during which he and the elders preached the gospel. God did a great work in the remote community and many of the people said they wanted to turn to Christ.

As they prepared to make the return trip one of the elders refused to leave the village. When asked why his reply was, "I will not return to Lome with you. I will stay here and teach these people God's Word. We cannot leave them without any teaching."

The elder did stay on and the director told me that there is a thriving church in that village today, and not only there, but in many surrounding villages of that region. The director himself had only arrived in Lome about one year earlier as a missionary from Nigeria and went home for one week once every three months to see his wife and children. Now the family was coming to join him in Lome. He had come in advance in order to have time to learn French before his family would come. Such is the dedication by many of these national missionaries.

The Lord had another surprise in store for me that day. We called at a local radio station and the station manager said he would see us in ten minutes. Eventually we were ushered into this very plush office where we found an executive surrounded by papers. I soon found out the manager was a lawyer and from this office he ran his business. The radio and television studios were behind his offices. From across his desk he began to share his testimony with me.

"When I was eight years old my parents became Jehovah's Witnesses. I went with them to the Kingdom Hall although I never thought of their faith for myself I finished school and trained as a high school teacher. I married, but soon we discovered that my wife could not bear children. We began looking for a solution, whether with 'white man's' medicine or with local herbs.

One day a pastor arrived and when my wife told him of her infertility he prayed that God would give us a child. Sure enough, by next year, my wife gave birth. When it came to the naming ceremony the pastor asked me to pray for something definite from the Lord and God would answer. I asked God to give me financial blessings, and if He did I would build a church.

I was studying law at the time and after obtaining my Master's degree became an attorney. The Lord answered prayer and I became rich. Unfortunately, I forgot my vow, and I began living the high life, moving with sophisticated girls, drinking, buying executive cars and building large houses to make lots of money. A year after becoming an attorney I became very sick. The doctors gave me all sorts of medicines, but to no avail. One day my friends took me to see the pastor who had prayed with my wife and for the first time I understood what my sins were and how Jesus could forgive my sins. That day I confessed my sins to God and asked the Lord Jesus into my life. God touched me that day and I was changed.

The pastor reminded me of the vow I had made some time ago when our child had been named. I bought some land and built the Baptist Gospel Church of Lome. After the inauguration of the church I was completely healed. Since that day God has helped me in so many ways, and it is a joy to be able to serve Him. I have since been able to build fifteen churches, but today rather than build buildings, I want to concentrate on spreading the good news. That is why I have purchased and outfitted two buses in which evangelists travel from village to village spreading the gospel. We have opened three radio stations and one television station here in Lome and run a medical centre, a missionary school and a home for the down and outs. I also head up a co-operative bank which helps our work. God is good to us, and I only want to please Him in my life."

He then went on to tell me that because he left witchcraft and a Masonic-like society he lost quite a few former clients, but he was not worried about that as God had provided many other clients and through his legal work he was able to finance the various works.

We further spoke of the spread of Islam in Togo and how governments impose high taxes on the Christian radio stations in the hope that this would discourage them from spreading the gospel.

I found the man so refreshing and it was evident he was burning out for God. When I shared with him the work of Every Home Crusade and how we could help him with evangelistic and follow-up literature he said that it was an answer to his prayers.

On that same journey Maizie related more of her experiences.

I arrived in Cotonou, capital of Benin and was told to take a taxi to the guesthouse which was supposed to be near the airport. When I emerged out of the arrival lounge I was confronted by almost fifty teenagers offering taxi rides. I saw an older man and thought it wiser to travel with him. After striking the right price I was taken to a taxi car, only to find it driven by a young lad. It had rained heavily before I arrived and the road was flooded in many places. When I saw the boy behind the steering wheel and imagined the slippery state of the roads I took a fit of giggling and said to myself, *Only in Africa.*

With my baggage in the boot, the driver removed a wet plastic bag from the passenger seat which was used to keep it dry from the water that poured in through the roof. The window on my side of the bone-shaker would neither open nor close so as we splashed through muddy puddles, I had an unwelcome but free shower. One headlight was at full beam, and one wiper only wiped a part of the windscreen. How he saw where he was going was a miracle, but he did not seem concerned. The most important thing to him was that his radio played at top volume. I only wished I had a video to record the reckless drive and miraculous arrival at my destination.

I have travelled to many cities all over Africa, but I have never seen traffic anywhere like that in Cotonou. I soon discovered that the cheapest and fastest way to get around the city was to hire a motorbike and a driver. At nearly all the traffic lights about sixty motorbikes of every size, shape and noise, were poised as if it was the start of a Grand Prix. As soon as the lights changed everyone beeped their horns and off they went. It seemed to be great for the motorcycle riders, but I assure you it was terrifying for a pillion passenger.

As I walked up a street I saw a white man exiting from a Land Rover on the side of which was a logo marked, Mercy Ships. I stopped with him to explain why I was in Cotonou and if their ship might be interested in EHC literature. He told me there were about four hundred people living on the ship, but he was the person responsible for the literature for their evangelistic programme. I visited the ship and found it most interesting. Locals received medical treatment free of charge. They had many specialised personnel for complicated surgeries including those who operated a cataract clinic.

Jacob, the leader of the Bible Study groups in Cotonou University heard that I had arrived with Christian literature and came to visit me at the guesthouse. The young man devoted all his time to the work among the students. He told me how he was raised in a Catholic home and went through all the religious ritual of his church. After school Jacob left for university where he met different religious groups, but was especially drawn to the voodoo schools. He told me that sixty per cent of the university students have allegiance to animistic gods. After being involved in voodoo for some time someone gave him a gospel tract. He read it over and over again and finally searched out the student who had given the tract to him. As a result he sought God's forgiveness and yielded His life to the Lord Jesus.

During the week he attended the University Bible Study, but at weekends he tried to fulfil his responsibilities towards his mother church. He found this to be very unsatisfactory. After discussing his problem with student friends he read the tract which taught that he needed to attend a church where Christ was presented as the only way of salvation. It was then that the light finally dawned on him how much he needed the fellowship of those who enjoyed like precious faith.

After he qualified as a teacher Jacob went on to teach in several colleges, but could never forget what God had taught him through the written word. As a result he dedicated his life to leading Bible studies and organising evangelistic events for students. When I shared with him the work of EHC he just kept thanking God for the possibility of having copies of the Gospel of John to give to these students.

Jacob was only one of several interesting people I met in Cotonou. I travelled from Cotonou to Lome by taxi for what they told me would be a four-hour journey. I sat in the front seat of the Peugeot 306 with four Africans squeezed into the back seat. It was a very hot morning when we set out and had only driven sixteen kilometres when a sudden surge of heat began to come from the engine. The driver stopped abruptly when he saw a rather hefty lady carrying several bags make her way towards the car. I knew that the only place for her was to share the seat with me, but I was at a loss to see how it could be done. I had been told that if I wanted the front seat to myself I would have to pay for two people. Seeing what might happen I swallowed my Ballymena reputation and suddenly became quite extravagant. I paid the driver for an extra place and was much relieved when he drove off and left the woman behind. She would catch the next taxi a few minutes later. The total cost was only £6.00, so I didn't feel too bad.

I could tell by their dress that the people in the rear seat were Muslims. When I discovered that the officials at the border were Muslims also, I just tagged along with my fellow passengers. As a result I got my passport stamped without any problem. The crossing at the actual border post was an unforgettable experience. People were roasting goats and chickens right there and offering meals to those crossing the border in both directions. Against the background of crowds of people milling around and a cacophony of noise from hens, roosters and goats, travellers kept shouting at the officials, "Am I next?" I was glad when we finally made it across the border into Togo.

On the dashboard of the taxi was written, "Maximum Speed 60 kph." The taxi driver took that as his minimum speed and used his horn constantly for at least one third of the journey. When I finally dismounted from the taxi several hours later, I was almost a nervous wreck. Time did not concern me. I was just glad to have arrived in one piece and gave thanks to the Lord for the fine work His angels had done to protect us. It really was a miracle!

The greater miracle was to follow. Tons of EHC literature followed to these West African countries and through the paper-missionaries and copies of the Gospel of John, thousands of lives have been touched. This has been a ministry of casting our bread upon the waters and in the eternal tabernacles of glory we shall see the miracles of grace which resulted from this work of faith.

The most recent report from Maizie gives further illustration of the power of the printed page.

As the teaching of the Branham cult spread throughout the Congo many of our church adherents who were weaker in the faith, joined up with the movement. Seminars were held almost daily in this new teaching and many with hungry hearts wanted to hear it for themselves. Many in the Congo do not possess God's Word and they felt this was a great opportunity to be taught. At the same time no one could ever question what these orators were saying, for they were quoting many Bible verses. Because these teachers quoted from the Bible a large section of people concluded their teachings must all be true.

Those who had been grounded in the Word could see many flaws in this new teaching and though they warned their "weaker brethren" to tread carefully, many were deceived and became loyal supporters of the Branhamist movement. Pastor Etape's heart was heavy as he watched some of his own people slide into this false teaching.

He set to pray for them and to write down on paper the errors of this teaching. As his burden grew greater he started to ask me if I could produce many copies of this little brochure on the errors of the Branhamist teaching. I discussed it with him, but in my heart of hearts I didn't really see it warranting a large production.

Thereafter, almost every time I met Pastor Etape he asked me the same question, "Have we made any progress on that tract?" It was really only in an effort to get him off my back that I discussed with the friends at EHC if it would be possible to produce this little leaflet. They were very keen to produce God's Word and thus help many of these "wayward folks." The printed tract duly arrived in the Congo and was especially distributed in the rural districts where the Branhamists had been busy.

While I was in Banalia I was attending the church service when opportunity was given to those who wanted to testify to God's goodness. This is not unusual in Congolese churches. A list is usually drawn up before the service to limit the number who might want to take part. A man stood up on this particular occasion and spoke of his first hearing the gospel and how he had been baptised in his local church. He told how the Branhamists came to them with all their promises of teaching seminars. Soon his whole family was swept along in this "new teaching." Still hungering to hear and learn more he gladly accepted a leaflet which had been handed to him and started to read it. Borrowing a Bible he began comparing what was written in the scriptures and what was being taught by the Branhamists. God was at work in His heart. The Psalmist declared years earlier, "The entrance of Thy Word giveth light" (Psalm 119:30). That light began to dawn upon this seeker of the truth.

As He read God slowly opened his understanding and here in the Banalia Church he was testifying that he had once "lost his way," but God had brought him back. After he spoke he asked his family to stand. Twenty-seven people stood up indicating that through the EHC tract they too had been delivered from this false cult.

In the New Testament epistle of James we read, "Let him know, that he which converteth the sinner from the error of his way shall save a soul from death, and shall hide a multitude of sins" (James 5:20). We praise God for the written word not only produced in all sixty-six books but also the many gospel leaflets which are available to us in the Lingala, Swahili, French and other languages used by the Congolese people. Every Home Crusade is a life line to many who are "wanting to hide His Word in their hearts."

When Samuel Adams travelled to the Congo in 1996 he had opportunity to visit various churches in Kisangani. He presumed that most of the Swahili literature that had been sent to the region some time prior to his visit had already been distributed. However, he was taken aback to discover a stockpile of boxes of tracts and booklets in a corner of one church. Keen to see the literature being used, Samuel tried to encourage the church leaders to circulate the literature as soon as possible. He was more than a little perplexed when the same leaders explained that they were holding this precious literature in reserve because they were not sure when they would receive another shipment from Every Home Crusade. Samuel assured them that he would dispatch another shipment from the Belfast factory as soon as he returned to Northern Ireland.

Samuel Adams did not know then that he would not be able to fulfil that promise. Because of the wars and the threats of war all large literature supplies had to be suspended for nine years. Every Home Crusade has responded to Maizie Smyth's urgent appeal to find a way of providing much needed literature for this region again. Great danger prevails in the region and the situation is unstable. However, even though it will be a lot more expensive, EHC is currently preparing to send an eighteen-tonne container full of gospel literature to Kampala in Uganda. From there the precious cargo will be transported to the Kisangani region by air.

These Congolese Christians are praying that they will not have to wait another nine years before they receive the Word of God in their own tongue. Every Home Crusade is committed to making sure that prayer will be answered.

# 11

## TRAVELLING IN THE LAND OF THE EAGLES
### *Cecil Gaw*

Who will ever forget the scenes in December, 1989 when "Peristroika" had its full effect? The Berlin Wall which divided Berlin city came tumbling down when people on both sides took up their picks and hammers and began to tear down that divisive and most hated wall in the world. The Iron Curtain, which had divided Eastern Europe from Western Europe for twenty-six years, was swept away in an unstoppable surge of liberation. For nearly a whole week people danced on the streets of Prague, Bucharest and Sofia as they celebrated the dawn of a new freedom after the long night of Soviet and communist oppression.

The overwhelming tide of emancipation seemed to be irresistible for the formerly closed countries. However, there was one country that was determined to resist "Peristroika". Albania! Albania was a bastion of communism where religion was outlawed, and God was considered to be persona-non-grata. For two years they held out while other surrounding nations enjoyed new liberty and prosperity.

Albania is about twice the size of Northern Ireland and has more than double Northern Ireland's population. The terrain is seventy-five per cent mountainous with some peaks towering up to 9,000ft. To Albanians their country is known as "Shqiperi" (the land of the eagles). Due to the strict policy of isolationism for nearly forty years, the country remained almost unknown to the rest of the world. Under the grim domination of its former dictator, Enver Hoxha, torture or execution were used to suppress independent thinking or expression. Because religion of all kinds was banned in Albania there were no Bibles, no Christian literature and no mention of God or the Lord Jesus Christ there.

Albania became the world's first official atheist state and flaunted a banner at the airport in Tirana, the capital, which proclaimed boldly: "In Albania there is no God". Thousands of Albanians who failed to conform to the dictatorship's rule were executed. As in other communist states, there was a huge Secret Police Force (the Sigurimi) and an intricate network of informers to ensure there was no deviation from the regime's oppressive policies. Economically, Albania became the poorest country in Europe and the prospect for the nation and its people looked bleak.

Albania's communist regime tried to outlaw God within its borders, but the Lord cannot be shut out. God declared that "all nations that he had made should come and worship before him" (Psalm 86:9). The Lord had other plans for this suppressed society. The notorious despot, Enver Hoxha, died in 1985, and the regime finally crumbled in 1991. This allowed the first beams of liberty and the light of the glorious gospel of Christ to shine into this once dark land. Even before Albania opened its borders God had been preparing some Christians to serve Him in that land. In countries as far apart as Italy and Australia, Mexico and England, USA and Northern Ireland, people were praying that Albania would open as a new sphere of service for God.

The opening of Albania's borders in 1991 forced many thousands of desperate Albanians to head for Italy in pursuit of relief from their economic distress.    Christian Assemblies in the south of Italy, associated with Gospel Halls in Northern Ireland, contacted a number of these people.  The Christians in the assemblies helped the refugees by providing them with practical aid and by telling them of the love of God and salvation through faith in the Lord Jesus.  As a result a number of these refugees were saved, and when they returned to their native country they invited the Italian believers to Albania to share the message of the gospel with their friends and relatives.

This request to enter Albania was not only a great answer to prayer, it also provided an effectual open door for the preaching of the gospel in that land.  Christian missionaries from assemblies in Italy and elsewhere soon answered the invitation and travelled to Albania to preach and teach the Word of God.  After years of spiritual famine the good seed of the Word fell on good soil and many Albanians, some of whom were hearing the gospel for the very first time, came to faith in Christ.  Subsequently, small assemblies were soon planted in different locations.  These believers promptly became very active in gospel outreach into the remote mountain villages where people had never heard the gospel or seen a Bible.

Cecil and Mildred Gaw, a couple from Belfast, visited Albania in May 1993.  While they were there they recognised the tremendous great need, both spiritual and physical, among the new and enthusiastic believers.  There were very few Bibles or New Testaments available in their own language and no access whatsoever to any helpful Christian literature. In addition, the Albanians they met were extremely poor and were living in difficult conditions, often without water or electricity.    It was clear to Cecil and Mildred that humanitarian aid was urgently required, as were large numbers of Bibles and Christian literature in the Albanian language, both for evangelical outreach and spiritual teaching.

On their return to Northern Ireland, Cecil reported to a number of interested assemblies in the province on what he and Mildred had witnessed in Albania. Many people were touched by the need and responded positively. They recognised that something needed to be done urgently to help this enthusiastic but ill-equipped Christian community.   In response the Albanian Christian Fund was set up. Wesley Ferguson from Antrim, David McNeill from Ballyclare and Cecil Gaw, who lives in Belfast, became the administrators of the Fund.

Not long after the Fund sent out its first newsletter outlining the dearth of appropriate Christian literature in Albania and the conditions of poverty in which many of the believers were living, generous Christians from Northern Ireland and elsewhere responded unstintingly.   Their continued liberality has allowed the Albanian Christian Fund (ACF) to help further the work of the Lord in many ways.

The provision of Christian literature has been a priority of the ACF, and in just over ten years they have supplied vast quantities to the Albanian church. This has included over 20,000 Bibles, well over 200,000 New Testaments and Gospel of John booklets and 200,000 copies of John Blanchard's booklet, *Ultimate Questions*, all written in Albanian. They have greatly appreciated the help of the Every Home Crusade in Belfast in printing one million copies of *Udha E Shpetimit* (The Way of Salvation), and 150,000 gospel booklets, *21st Century, What Should You Believe and Who Can You Trust*.   Every Home Crusade, along with the Trinitarian Bible Society, has also produced and made available hundreds of thousands of attractive Albanian gospel calendars to be distributed throughout the country.

Humanitarian aid has also been a very important part of the work of the ACF for the last number of years. The Scriptures state, "Blessed is he that considers the poor" (Psalm 41:1). The margin of my Bible enlarges on the word "poor" as those who are "sick and weak". This scripture has been an encouragement to all those involved in this aspect of the social aspect of this ministry. Nearly every year since it was established ACF has sent out at least three forty-five-foot, eighteen wheeler trucks packed with shoes, clothes, bedding, food, medical supplies, and a variety of other different items that have been specifically requested by the Albanian believers. Because transport costs are high ACF has asked that only new, washed, or dry-cleaned clothes be given. Furthermore, it is preferable that everything donated and sent out should be of good quality.

An army of willing Christian volunteers gladly devote their time and energy to ensure the efficient sorting of the donated material and the packing of the trucks. Everything that has been sent so far has arrived safely and has been distributed by Christians who are known and trusted. In addition to the aid sent out in trucks, ACF has supplied and assumed responsibility for the maintenance of ten vehicles, most of which are new Land Rovers. When the administrators of the Fund travel out to Albania they use discretion to provide financial help where they see an immediate need.

The Albanian believers and the missionaries there have greatly appreciated the love and care that has been shown to them over the years. In the reports of the ACF are many extracts out of letters they have received expressing profound gratitude for all they have done.

Cecil and Mildred Gaw have made twenty-two visits to Albania since 1993, and Cecil has had the privilege of preaching the gospel in halls and in the remote mountain villages. Cecil has also endeavoured to learn the language and has mastered it sufficiently to allow him to preach for about twenty minutes in Albanian. The locals find it amusing to hear their language being spoken with a Northern Ireland accent! It has been rewarding to see souls saved as a result of his preaching, and Cecil and Mildred pray that others who have heard the message might even yet come to know the Saviour.

The Lord has protected and preserved them as they have driven a Land Rover over many difficult and dangerous mountain tracks. Despite the hardships, Cecil reckons it is worth it all. He said, "It is a wonderful privilege to preach the gospel to mountain villagers who have never heard anything about our wonderful Saviour, the Lord Jesus Christ." During a visit in October 2004 they were thrilled when the son of a Muslim priest told them how he had gone home after hearing the gospel, confessed his sin and accepted the Lord Jesus Christ as his Saviour.

Wesley and Joan Ferguson and David and May McNeill, the other administrators and their wives, have accompanied Cecil and Mildred on some of their trips to Albania. The Albanian Christians hold all these couples in high esteem. Cecil finds it refreshing to have Wesley and David to help him, not only with the preaching and Bible teaching opportunities, but also with identifying the most pressing needs and distributing funds accordingly.

However, as it is often the case when the work of God is prospering, all the forces of evil seem to gang up against it. This was the Apostle Paul's experience when describing his work to the Christians in Corinth in a letter he said, "A great door and effectual is opened unto me, and there are many adversaries" (1 Corinthians 16:9).

In 1997 there was a period of unrest in the country, during which Cecil and Mildred were held up several times by armed men. They proved that in times of trouble God is a very ready help and they were not harmed.

Seventy per cent of Albanians are nominal Muslims. In recent years, Islamic missionaries have been trying to convert them to a more fundamental form of Islam. Over one thousand mosques have been constructed during the last decade. Besides this, many false cults have arrived in the country, Mormons and Jehovah's Witnesses being amongst the most active. There is also some persecution of Christians who openly confessed their faith in Christ. This abuse is most prevalent in the mountain villages where it is considered disloyal to turn your back on the religion of your forefathers.

The work of God continues to flourish however, despite all the opposition, and those responsible for the Albanian Christian Fund are pledged to carry on supporting it as guided by the Lord. It is their prayer that the believers whom they have come to know and love in the "land of the eagles" may have the same experience of God as his ancient people, Israel. During their trials God "bare you on eagles' wings, and brought you unto myself" (Exodus 19:4).

# 12

## TEACHING THE WORD IN A TROUBLED WORLD
### *Eric and Anne Magowan*

"Jump on the back of this motor-cycle, and I'll have you at the class in a few minutes," the driver told Eric Magowan. Eric covered his mouth and nose with an anti-air-pollution mask, put on his crash helmet, grabbed his back-pack and settled on the rear saddle behind the spirited motorcyclist. The friendly believer from a Far Eastern country (his name cannot be given) competed with similar motor bikes as he weaved in and out through the city's heavily congested morning traffic. Eric was glad for the security of a crash helmet after a few near-collisions. He thought of those back home who were praying for his protection and thanked the Lord for answering their prayers.

Here and there Eric spied uniformed policemen and wondered if they were watching him and his companion. At least, he felt the crash helmet might hide his identity. Just then it struck Eric that he needed something more important than a crash helmet; it was imperative that the Lord preserve him and the believers he was going to meet from the intervention of the heavy-handed authorities. Eric prayed that the Lord would frustrate any possible scrutiny by the authorities.

After a fifty minute trip Eric was grateful when they safely arrived at a house located on one of the city's back streets. There were no obvious indications that any students had turned up for a seminar. There were no bicycles, no motor scooters and not even a car in sight. However, when Eric entered the inconspicuous meeting place he was greeted by more than thirty-five students with beaming smiles and cheery greetings to welcome their teacher. Some of these students had travelled a considerable distance to be there, some had been on the road over four days. Others had already spent time in prison because they had chosen to follow Jesus Christ and serve Him in spite of the opposition from communist authorities.

After the initial welcome and introductions, Eric was able to matriculate each pastor and evangelist. He had to be careful not to retain any written record of their names or their addresses. The students then settled down to business, a consolidated week of Bible teaching in this ministry seminar. As Eric taught the Word of God the students seemed to absorb the material like a sponge. Eric was conscious that he was involved in preparing these servants of God for the building of His church in their troubled and persecuted country. Just as a lion knows that the best place to pounce on his prey is at a watering hole, so the devil lurks near to where God's people are being fed. We must never forget that the devil is aware that this Bible teaching ministry is vital, and therefore he never tires of trying to disrupt this work. Many times the police have come to where the students were studying, but each time God has miraculously spared his children and they have been out of the building before the police arrived. They really do believe that the "angel of the Lord encampeth round about them that fear him, and delivereth them" (Psalm 34:7).

A great conflict still persists in this region of Asia which has been no stranger to warfare. Since the communists took control of the whole country, the church of Jesus Christ has been growing at a parallel rate to that experienced in China. Besides thousands of believers who belong to established liberal churches, a greater number of new Christians meet in unregistered house churches. Many believe these to be the true evangelical back bone of the Church of Christ in that land. In an attempt to suppress this growth and spiritual awakening, the communist government has been persecuting believers, imprisoning pastors and evangelists and bringing false charges against key leaders of the Christian church. The main reason for this persecution is because the authorities cannot intimidate or control these believers. Not even by meting out cruel torture can these authorities induce Christians to recant or deny the Lord Jesus as their Saviour.

The pastors and evangelists who attend Eric's seminars have never been outside their country and have little or no formal theological training. Furthermore, they have no worthwhile libraries and very few personal resources to help develop their ministries. Foreign missionaries from Asia and beyond make frequent, but short-stay excursions, into the country to meet, encourage and teach seminars for these Christian workers. Some missionaries represent well-known Bible schools and theological institutions, which offer degree courses to pastors and each seminar carries merits for the respective course.

After serving God in Africa for more than twenty-three years with UFM Worldwide, Eric and Anne Magowan caught the vision of travelling to Asia in 1997 in order to help the persecuted church. It was a big transition in their lives, but let us go back to the beginning to see how it all began.

Eric Magowan was raised in the Bessbrook area of South Armagh. During a Faith Mission evangelistic outreach at the Christian Workers Union in Bessbrook, Eric responded to the claims of the gospel when he was still at the tender age of fourteen. Through peer pressure at school and during his adolescent years Eric drifted away from his initial conversion for several years. However, on 20th November 1964, he came back to the Saviour at special meetings at Mourne Presbyterian Church in Kilkeel, conducted by the late Rev. Tom Rees of Hildenborough Hall in Kent.

Anne McCloy was raised in a Christian home in East Belfast and gave her heart to the Lord Jesus as a young child. Besides the influence of her Christian parents, Anne also benefited greatly from the faithful Bible teaching at Glenburn Gospel Hall and the Iron Hall where the family attended. Anne's father maintains that since her childhood, Anne was always very serious in her Christian life, and he wasn't surprised when the Lord called her into full-time Christian service.

It was evident that God had His hand upon both Eric and Anne from an early age. After Anne left school she gained employment in the Northern Ireland Civil Service at the Ministry of Commerce. Meanwhile, Eric took up a career as a motor mechanic at C. R. Morrow's garage in his hometown. Although Eric felt he had chosen his career, he was unaware that it was God who was preparing him for what lay ahead. The eight years Eric invested as a motor mechanic in Armagh was not only very useful employment, but would be a most beneficial, if not an essential skill in the heart of Africa in later years.

Eric Magowan and Anne McCloy did not meet each other until they both attended the annual UFM Young People's Missionary Conference in Larne during the spring of 1965. That conference was to change their lives completely. Not only did the young couple meet, become good friends and begin a tentative relationship, it was also as a result of the missionary challenge at the conference that they, with many other young people, responded to dedicate their lives to the Lord for missionary service.

That conference was memorable for other reasons. It came just after the 1964 Belgian Congo Simba Rebellion when many missionaries and their children were massacred and others were taken captive. An appeal was made at the Larne conference to answer the challenge and for young people to offer their lives as new missionaries to replace those who had paid the ultimate price of martyrdom. Eric and Anne surrendered their lives to God for whatever He might have for them. They could never have imagined what that would be.

Having struck up their initial friendship during that weekend conference, Eric and Anne began to meet each other periodically and go out together. Neither was sure if this relationship was the Lord's will for their lives, and they were hesitant to persist in any commitment to each other in case they should miss God's best for their lives.

Eric and Anne waited on the Lord for His guidance, they prayed together and shared with each other how God was dealing with their lives. By 1968 the sense of call to the Lord's work had not abated, and both felt it was time to consider going to Bible college. Anne was guided to the Bible Training Institute in Glasgow. However, before going she and Eric terminated their relationship so they could be open to God's guidance for their lives. With her eye still on the mission field, Anne made full use of her two-year course at Bible College.

Eric went to the opposite end of the country when he enrolled for the three-year course at South Wales Bible College in Barry, near Cardiff. He also applied himself to his studies during those three years without the distraction of a romance or commitment to marriage. However, the longer he studied and the more he viewed the work God was calling him to, Eric realised that he would need the girl of God's choice at his side. He committed this to God in prayer.

After completing two years in Glasgow Anne was constrained to apply to Child Evangelism Fellowship for more training and practical experience. She was glad for the opportunity to put her new-found skills into operation while working with CEF missionaries among the boys and girls in county Fermanagh. This experience greatly enriched Anne's life and would later prove to be a great benefit to her ministry in Africa.

Through all their training the young couple were constant in their focus to what God had put in their hearts. There was never any doubt in their minds that God was leading them to Africa. They knew this was a lifetime commitment and there could be no turning back. With such a single-minded focus in their lives Eric and Anne re-established their relationship, and in December 1970, before Eric finished his course at the South Wales Bible College, they became engaged to be married.

During that final year of Eric's training the newly engaged couple completed their application to Unevangelised Fields Mission for the work in the Congo. After a series of interviews they were accepted as candidates for that work. Eric and Anne determined to place no limits on how long they would be in Africa or make any deals with God as to how they would serve Him. Furthermore, at that time no one spoke of visits to the Africa to see if they would like the place or not before their final commitment to the work. Eric and Anne were totally committed to what God had in store for them. They were trusting Him completely and knew there could be no half measures with God. It was their all or nothing.

Eric completed his training at South Wales Bible College in June 1971, and the happy couple were married in the Iron Hall on 3rd August, 1971. Three weeks after their wedding the new Mr. & Mrs. Eric Magowan headed off to Albertville in France to commence language study.

After a year of language study Eric and Anne returned to Northern Ireland to raise their support and prepare for going to Africa. On 11th April, 1973 Eric and Anne finally left the shores of Northern Ireland for the Congo, which by that time had changed its name to Zaire (the name reverted to the Democratic Republic of Congo at the end of the 1990s).

Their first four-year term seemed to go by very quickly, but it was not without its heartaches and problems. Bongondza, their first station, was a remote town located over one hundred and sixty miles into the vast forest. It took sixteen laborious hours to reach the town by Land Rover. It was a rough ride over a primitive road, which was peppered with massive craters, and deep potholes in dry season and became a quagmire during the wet season.

The Mission Hospital at Bongondza had been severely damaged by the 1964 war of the Simba Rebellion and was still in a state of extreme disrepair. As soon as they got there Anne began her work at the hospital pharmacy, while Eric attended to many practical assignments which demanded his attention daily. This involved repairs to the hospital building, installation of generators to provide electricity for the hospital, digging wells and plumbing to supply running water for the hospital and surrounding homes. Eric also worked with some locals to clear the forest and provide a safe airstrip for the Missionary Aviation Fellowship plane, which provided vital services for the missionaries and hospital at Bongondza. Added to all this activity, they were careful to attend to the main purpose for which they gone to Zaire, the ministry of the gospel to the boys and girls and men and women of that region.

Anne was able to organise children's meetings, supervise Sunday schools and give Religious Instruction classes at the day-schools in the town. Meanwhile, Eric engaged in preaching the gospel at the brick-built church on the mission station as well as at many of the smaller churches in the surrounding forest. Early on Sunday mornings Eric and Anne often headed off in the Land Rover with ten or twelve evangelists and elders on board. They dropped the preachers off at various villages along the way as they made their way to the end of the line. Services and conferences were conducted at all these preaching points. Later in the day the preachers were all picked up for the return journey to Bongondza.

Eric and Anne discovered after some time of working on the field that there was a great necessity for gospel literature, but a great lack of suitable material. The people had no television as a distraction, and many of them had learned to read and they were hungry to read anything and everything. Often they would walk long distances just to acquire some reading material. The Magowans were frustrated that Christian literature was so expensive and hard to come by in their isolated area. Sadly they didn't have access to the ministry of Every Home Crusade in those early days.

During this period in Bongondza Eric and Anne were over the moon when they discovered that Anne was expecting their first baby. Sadly, that happiness and their hopes were tragically dashed when their little daughter was stillborn. It was with heavy hearts that they buried the little infant at the Bongondza station. For the next few months Anne underwent several small operations at Nyankunde hospital. This was followed by a time of needed rest and convalescence. It took some time before Anne was able to make sufficient recovery to be able to engage in the ministry that she loved.

While working at Bongondza God led Eric and Anne into a teaching and encouragement ministry for the many untrained pastors and evangelists in that region. Most of these Christian workers had never been to a Bible school, and their wives were expected to play the part of a pastor's wife, giving leadership to the women and children's ministries in the churches. For this new ministry Eric installed electric light in the church and conducted pastoral-training and the Bible classes every Wednesday afternoon and evening. Anne also provided teacher-training classes for the women to better equip them to be able to lead the children and ladies' ministry in their churches.

After two very worthwhile years at Bongondza, Eric and Anne were requested by the Zairian church to move to the city of Kisangani. Their move to this city was followed by the birth of their son Gareth. Kisangani provided Eric and Anne with an opportunity of an even greater ministry than they had experienced in Bongondza. Instead of just a training class for local pastors and evangelists, the African Church leaders wanted them to extend this ministry to the rest of the churches in the UFM region. This new ministry involved a great deal of travelling from area to area, covering hundreds of miles over slippery and precarious roads, and all this with a new-born baby in arms. However, it was a very rewarding and encouraging ministry. It gave Eric and Anne great joy to see the positive response of the pastors and their wives, many of whom travelled hundreds of miles, trekked for many days, just to attend the seminar and study the Word of God. The one thing that disappointed and frustrated Eric and Anne the most was the lack of suitable evangelistic literature and Bible study material to leave with these Christian workers

When their furlough came around in 1981 Eric and Anne resolved that they would have to do something about the dearth of Christian literature before they would return to the Congo for their next term of service. It was during that year at home that they became acquainted with the work of Every Home Crusade. After a meeting with Mr. Ernie Allen and Mr. Samuel Adams they were greatly excited when these men consented to provide the Magowans with some much needed literature. Eric took time to translate various booklets and tracts into Lingala and Bangala. Eric and Anne knew that the literature would be very useful in their ministry and greatly appreciated by the African Church. This was just the beginning of Eric and Anne's long association with Every Home Crusade factory in Belfast and the team of workers employed there.

When they returned to Zaire in 1982 Eric and Anne were posted several hundred miles farther north from Kisangani to establish the Bangala Bible School in Poko. This region was mainly under the leadership of Worldwide Evangelisation Crusade (WEC) missionaries who gladly shared the work with their colleagues from UFM. Before leaving Northern Ireland Eric and Anne were overjoyed to know that twelve tea chests full of Every Home Crusade literature in the Lingala, Bangala, Swahili and French languages, were sent to Zaire ahead of them and hopefully, would be there for their arrival.

One obstacle to be overcome was the transportation of this literature across Kenya and Uganda into Zaire. Although Eric had given some thought to the matter he need never have worried for the Lord had gone before them and prepared the way. For the mutual benefit of missionary endeavour in Africa there is usually very good cross cultural co-operation between evangelical missions and missionaries. In order to help the Magowans on this occasion the missionaries of the German Mission, Diguna, offered to transport the literature free of charge to Zaire on their big truck which was frequently used on this hazardous journey. The only request the German missionaries made was that Eric and Anne share some of the tea chests of literature with them. Not only were the Magowans happy to agree to their request, they were also glad to put the Diguna Mission in touch with Every Home Crusade so that they would be able to receive their own shipments of literature. Since then the Diguna missionaries have been receiving container loads of EHC literature periodically.

An interesting incident happened on the first occasion the Diguna truck transported the literature from Kenya to Zaire. After the truck departed Eric followed a day later in his Land Rover. At the Zairian border Eric noticed a border guard sitting reading a copy of the *"Way of Salvation"* booklet in the Bangala language. When Eric approached the soldier to ask if he understood what he was reading, the soldier looked up at Eric with a measure of guilt written all over his face. He immediately tried to hide the booklet inside his uniform and began to deny he had any booklet. It was obvious that the sense of guilt was because the soldier had stolen the booklet from one of the tea chests that he had searched when the truck crossed the border the previous day. Eric smiled as he mused, "God has many ways of spreading his Word."

Eric took time to explain to the embarrassed soldier that he had translated the booklet from English into Bangala and just like the gospel of Jesus Christ, the booklets were free of charge. Even though the soldier continued to listen to the gospel message he couldn't bring himself to admit that he had pilfered the booklet from the truck. Eric prayed that the man would later understand what he was reading.

Eric and Anne believe that the ten years they spent at the Poko Bible College were probably the most enjoyable and profitable years they spent in Africa. Baby Gareth was just three years old when they arrived there and his little sister Estelle was born in that remote region eighteen months after they arrived there. Poko was even more remote than Bongondza. Their nearest town, Isiro, was over ninety miles away and it took them at least sixteen hours to drive there, provided there were no breakdowns, trees across the road or old broken-down trucks blocking the single lane road to town.

At the Bible School Eric directed a three-year training course for about forty young couples with a fresh intake of new students on alternate years. Most of these students returned to their own communities which were buried deep into the forest, to pastor their own people in simple churches. Anne taught the women in children and women's ministries, how to be a pastor's wife and how to be a help to their husband's ministry.

Because many of these students could barely read or write it was necessary that the course work be simple and crystal-clear. One thing was certain, in spite of their poverty and lack of education, the students had a clear "call" from the Lord to serve Him and they came with a great determination to learn and study God's Word.

Anne had to teach many of them to read and write in their own language before they were able to study the Bible. All over Africa the people have such a great hunger to read. Once they acquire a little competence in reading they will read just about everything they can get their hands on. This leaves them very vulnerable to false teachings. It was therefore, a great blessing for Eric and Anne to put the Word of God into their hands.

Throughout the world false cults abound and are very diligent in propagating their erroneous teachings, deluding thousands of people who are easily beguiled by their insidious and persuasive words. It should also be noted that the most effective instrument these cults employ is the use of the printed page in very attractive tracts, booklets and books. Not only are some gullible and unsuspecting people taken in by these false teachings, but many sincere but unlearned believers can fall foul to these false movements. New believers often don't know the difference between the truth and the false teachings and therefore mistakenly suppose that because the literature speaks of Jesus Christ it must be true. For that reason the missionaries praise God for Every Home Crusade and other evangelical agencies whose literature can be relied upon for publishing the truth of the scriptures and the scriptures of truth.

During three twelve-week terms each year these young men and women in the Poko Bible College were grounded in the scriptures every day. Eric taught the men how to preach and teach the Word, while Anne gave her emphasis to the ladies on their ministry in the church. These students reproduced what they were taught by returning to their churches to train Sunday school teachers and other workers in their respective congregations. In this way God's work in the bush grew and multiplied at an amazing rate.

Nothing gave Eric and Anne more joy than being part of the Bible school work when the students were sent out every Sunday into the forest on bicycles, on foot or sometimes taken by Land Rover, to evangelise the lost and encourage isolated believers. They were such a happy bunch of young students, and they had happy times trekking or cycling along a multitude of forest trails to fulfil the Lord's command to "Go and teach all nations."

There was equal joy on Monday mornings when the workers returned to class to report and praise God for the dozens of souls who had trusted Christ during the previous day. There were so many exciting stories to tell of the places they visited, the people they met, the things that happened to them, the sermons they preached and how the literature was distributed. There were also requests for prayer when they returned with burdens on their hearts for sad situations they met or when things did not go as they had hoped.

It was not uncommon to discover that there was not one Bible in many of the villages. Bibles were not easily obtained and when they were available they were so expensive that the price was beyond what these poor people could afford. Many people in the western society may not be so quick to buy the scriptures if a Bible cost what was equal to a month or two month's wages. That is what it would have cost a man in the bush if he was left to purchase the scriptures without the subsidy of the missionary. In the absence of a Bible, the Every Home Crusade literature was the only portion of the scriptures the people had until Eric and Anne were able to obtain Bibles for them.

The *"Way of Salvation"* booklet was a great favourite with these isolated believers because it contained selected scripture passages from throughout the Bible and yet provided a bird's-eye view of the whole Bible. One incident stands out in Eric and Anne's memory.

In 1982 the Christmas Makatano (Christmas Conference) was held about 150 miles north of Poko at another Church station. There were no resident missionaries at Makatano.
Most of the students had been allocated to where they should to go for the Christmas vacation. Vacation for the students is not a holiday time. During these weeks when the students were out of school they were expected to engage in evangelistic outreach. Local pastors were always keen for a

few married couples to help them during the Christmas vacation. Some of the students joined Eric and Anne's family to travel by Land Rover to the Central Makatano.

The Christmas Conference was an annual event although it changed from one station to another each year. Up to five thousand people from a hundred mile radius gathered for the conference which lasted from 24th December through to the 2nd January for a great time of gospel outreach and Bible teaching ministry.

I had been scheduled to preach once or twice every day and was especially responsible for the main service, which began on Christmas morning at 9.00am. and went right through until 1.00pm. It turned out to be an unforgettable day for all who were there.

I had sought the Lord for a Christmas message, and it seemed He kept bringing me back to Exodus 20:8, "Remember the Sabbath day to keep it Holy." It did not seem to be a likely Christmas text but there was such an impression laid upon my heart that I felt compelled by God to preach on that verse.

On that Christmas morning, shortly after I began to preach, a "black mamba", one of Africa's most deadly and poisonous snakes, dropped down from the bamboo and palm-branch roof which covered the conference building. It caused great panic among the people. One saintly lady, who was eighty years old and had travelled from Poko with us, jumped up and called out, "Don't let Satan into our meeting!"

Someone quickly killed the snake, and everyone settled back for the rest of the service. Very soon it became obvious that this was no ordinary meeting. The presence of God became a felt reality. Services and sermons in Africa are better measured by their length than by their depth. People calculate that there is no point in walking fifteen or twenty miles for a twenty minute sermon. However, such was the presence of the Lord in that meeting that hardly anybody noticed that I had been preaching for nearly three hours. The Lord was among His people, and no one was in any hurry.

Just as I was about to conclude the message, I noticed from the corner of my eye dozens of people streaming up the road toward our palm-roofed structure. Suddenly, someone inside the church stood to their feet crying out to God in deep repentance and pleading for forgiveness of their sins. Then another person stood up and cried unto God for mercy. This was followed by yet another man on his feet calling on God for forgiveness. Within a short time the whole place erupted with cries of deep anguish and brokenness which accompanied their deep repentance to God. Some people were even pouring dust and ashes over their heads as a sign of their mourning. Some were begging others for forgiveness and putting things right with their family members, friends and neighbours.

I could do nothing but seek the Lord and pray with those who were near to me. I was particularly struck that although so much was happening, there was no confusion or disorder among the people, nor were they babbling in tongues. There was just a true brokenness and genuine repentance before God. I remember hearing that in the earlier revivals in the Congo, "Repentance is the sign of genuine revival." These people meant business with God!

That was the end of the official schedule for that Christmas Day. During the rest of the day and through the whole night, soft cries of anguish could be heard. This was followed by the sounds of joy as people found peace and forgiveness. About five hundred people sought and found faith in Jesus Christ that day. Many of these new converts had never even heard the gospel message before. They were greatly overcome with a deep sense of conviction of sin and therefore, came to the church building to find an answer to their agony of soul.

Some other seekers came hurriedly running along the road. They were anxious to get right with God, but they arrived at

the church just before dawn broke only to find that the service
had finished. It was obvious to all that the message from the
scriptures and the moving of the Holy Spirit had drawn many
hearts to God. The living Lord Jesus was moving amongst
us.

Needless to say, every piece of literature we had was used up
during that conference, and we did not find one page that was
thrown away. Every tract and booklet was taken home to be
read and re-read and then shared and explained to others.

God's little paper missionaries did their job that day, finding
their way into many homes where no white man would ever
enter. The most important thing of all is for God's Word to
reach into the depths of man's soul to a place where the mere
words of man could never penetrate.

A few years later the Magowans were moved to Bunia, a border
town in north-eastern Congo and than later to Nairobi in Kenya. While
in Nairobi Eric received several eighteen-tonne containers from Every
Home Crusade to be used all over East and Central Africa. Even then
Eric found it difficult to keep up with the demands of the evangelists
and pastors who were trying to supply scripture portions for those who
had a great hunger for reading God's Word.

Since returning to Northern Ireland in 1995 Eric and Anne have
been constantly involved in the work of UFM Worldwide. They have
made repeated visits to Africa, one with Samuel Adams to review, help
and encourage the church in Congo. Their son Gareth, trained to be a
pilot in USA and for several years has been flying in the East Africa
region, including into Congo, where he provides a service to
missionaries in some of the places he knew when growing up in
Africa.

In 1997 the Lord opened the door for Eric to travel to Eastern Asia
where he was overwhelmed with the hunger for Bible teaching and
need to help Pastors and Christian workers in that region. As a result
Eric has since opened his covert Bible School training and support
ministry in a closed communist country. To date Eric has made almost

thirty trips to this troubled and closed land and more than one hundred and forty pastors and evangelists have benefited from the training course. God has made this opportunity possible by the backup help of those who support the ministry with their generous giving and commitment to prayer for Eric and Anne.

# 13

# A NEW VISION FOR EUROPE'S MILLIONS
## *Tom and Margaret Somerville*

"Dad, here is something just for you," said Jane with all the exuberance and willingness of youth as she pushed a missionary circular into her Dad's hand. Jane had just returned from three months as a volunteer worker at Child Evangelism Fellowship's headquarters in Kilchzimmer, Switzerland and was consequently sold out on the idea of reaching Europe's children with the gospel. Tom, Jane's dad, read the lines his daughter had indicated, "Financial adviser required for work in Kilchzimmer."

Tom was already a member of the local Fermanagh CEF Council and shared his daughter's enthusiasm and vision to reach boys and girls. *A financial advisor in Switzerland?* Tom mused. As manager of the Ulster Bank in Lisnakea Tom was certainly qualified for the assignment. Furthermore, as a Christian, Tom, since his conversion several years earlier, had been involved with and committed to reaching others with the gospel of Jesus Christ. As he pondered the possibility of going to Kilchzimmer and talked the matter over with his wife, Margaret, what might have seemed improbable or foolish to any other person in his secure position, began to become a distinct probability. Tom felt he had already wasted too many years of his life since he wasn't converted until he was in his mid-thirties.

Tom Somerville was born into a Christian home in Tandragee, County Armagh just before the end of the Second World War. However, when Tom was only a toddler, his father who often preached in nearby churches, died quite suddenly. Mrs. Somerville learned to lean more and more on God during those early days of widowhood with three young children.

Sadly, young Tom did not follow in his mother's footsteps. Although he was sent to Sunday School and taken to church regularly, when he entered his early teens he rebelled against Christianity and the restrictions it seemed to impose on his life and ambitions. He felt he knew a better way to live -- a way that did not include God or Jesus Christ.

Through those adolescent years and into adulthood Tom pursued his own ways and greatly indulged in the pleasures of the world. He secured a good job, which provided him with a fairly good income, an enjoyable life-style and a good car. Tom met and married Margaret who came from Portadown. They bought a house and settled down to have their family. While married Tom left the housekeeping business to Margaret, and he continued to enjoy regular social activities with his friends.

By the time Tom emerged into his mid-thirties he became very disenchanted with his life and lifestyle. Although he had gained promotion in his job, had sufficient money, plenty of earthly possessions, a good wife and three beautiful children, Tom felt there was something missing in his life. When he hit the age of thirty-five Tom calculated that half of his life was over, and he had failed to find any lasting joy, satisfaction or contentment. He concluded that another thirty-five years of empty living would break his heart and would probably result in his life falling apart.

He turned these matters over in his mind, and he remembered his mother, his childhood and the truths he was taught in Sunday School and church. Tom felt there had to be another way to live, a better way. It was God's way. Tom confessed, "I knew of this other way. Maybe that was the answer. I thought I would begin by examining this other way and see what it had to offer. I had always had many deep questions about life, which had never been answered. Questions like, *'What am I here for?'* *'Is man made only for this life?'* It cannot be. If so, then life is futile. There must be something after this life. There must be a way to find satisfaction in this life."

At thirty-five years old Tom began then to read the Bible for the first time in his life. He started in the New Testament, and as he read through Matthew he discovered that not only was he reading the Bible, the Bible was reading Tom Somerville. He became aware of the depth and reality of his sin and discovered that he was a slave to sinful lusts. It seemed as if he had been living in a prison of his small world drawn as a circle around him. Tom also discovered that there was One, and only One, who could set him free from sin, the Lord Jesus Christ. It was at the beginning of 1979 that Tom bowed to his knees and cried, "Lord, I'm tired of my sin. It's a great burden. I'm deeply ashamed of my life. Lord, I come to you. Please save me, Lord."

Years later while lying in a hospital bed Tom recalled the impact of his conversion on his life, "All things changed. My life, our home, my family -- it all changed. It was never the same again, thank God. There was a new song in my heart. Even the very creation seemed new as though I hadn't really seen it before. It was breathtaking. I felt free for the first time in my life. That same year, my wife and three daughters, then aged four, seven and ten, also came to trust and love the Lord Jesus. Since then we have had two more daughters who also received the Saviour into their lives."

Tom and Margaret were living in Crumlin at the time of his conversion. Immediately he got involved in the work of the local Presbyterian Church where Rev. Brian Kennaway was the minister. He thoroughly enjoyed Brian's contagious enthusiasm for the work among young people, and Tom threw himself wholeheartedly into this work.  At the peak of his involvement in the Crumlin Church, Tom was transferred to Irvinestown in Co. Fermanagh.

While settling into life in Ulster's lakeland county Tom and Margaret pursued finding a good local church to attend.  A good friend, the late David Strachan, recommended they try the Colaghty Parish Church near Lack.  They soon got to know the Rector, Rev. Bertie Johnston, who encouraged their interest and involvement with young people and children. Under Rev. Johnston's ministry Tom and Margaret developed deeply in their Christian lives.  They learned so much they felt they had been to Bible College.  Added to this, Tom was invited to be part of the local Child Evangelism Fellowship Committee while the girls enjoyed the benefit of CEF camps both in Fermanagh and elsewhere.

It was after their daughter Jane's three months visit as a volunteer worker at CEF's headquarters in Kilchzimmer, Switzerland that she challenged Tom to consider plying his accounting skills for the benefit of CEF Europe. Challenges often come at crucial times and this was the case with Tom and Margaret. Plans were well under way for building a new house in Fermanagh. Tom did not want anything to distract him from God's purpose. He wanted his life and time to count for Jesus Christ. However, he had never thought that this might involve stepping out to serve CEF in a full-time capacity. He discovered that as he prayed about the need in Kilchzimmer, a deep conviction settled on his heart that he should pursue this step.

After consultation with Sam Doherty, the European director of CEF at that time, Tom and Sam concluded that he was not suited for the vacancy in Kilchzimmer. However, Sam Doherty could see that Tom's skills and experience would be a great asset to God's work in Europe.  Sam asked Tom and Margaret to consider another possibility. CEF work in Eastern Europe needed a co-ordinator for their office in Vienna, Austria.  Sam was sure that Tom and Margaret were ideal to fill that role.

After much prayer and consideration, Tom and Margaret surrendered their lives to God for the work in Eastern Europe and on

14th February, 1990 they embarked on a deputation tour to raise support and awareness for their venture to Vienna. During Tom's thirty years in the bank he had lived in five of Northern Ireland's six counties, so he was able to travel widely to share with friends what God was doing in his life.

It was a major upheaval for Tom at forty-seven years of age and for the whole Somerville family. It was agreed that the three older daughters would remain at home while the nine-year-old twins, Rachel and Ruth, would accompany their mum and dad to Austria. They left Northern Ireland in August 1991.

Settling into a continental capital was a whole new experience for the family. Rachel and Ruth were enrolled in a local German speaking school, while Tom and Margaret became better acquainted with their Eastern European co-workers and their respective works. By this time Eastern Europe had been liberated from the former Soviet domination and there were great opportunities to reach boys and girls throughout the region.

On a visit to Sibiu in central Romania, Tom was further challenged by the great need and opportunity for child evangelism in that city and the surrounding area. His number of visits to Romania increased, and he generally spent a period of two to three weeks in the country at a time. Roy Harrison, the successor of Sam Doherty as European Director of CEF, asked Tom and Margaret to consider moving from Austria to Sibiu to help in the growing CEF programme.

Within a short time in Sibiu Tom saw a great opportunity to reach millions of children through special literature designed for boys and girls. CEF USA had introduced the MailBox Club as a means to recruit children for Bible correspondence courses. The programme proved to be very successful in the United States and some of their tracts were translated into the Romanian language. These tracts were then widely distributed in central Romania and brought an immediate response. Dozens of boys and girls contacted Tom and his co-workers to subscribe for the course.

This overwhelming response gave Tom an understanding of the potential of using literature to reach the millions of children in

Romania. The quantity of literature received from USA was insufficient, and it was unlikely that more would follow. As he thought and prayed about the matter and where he might be able to obtain suitable leaflets his mind drifted to the work of the Every Home Crusade in Belfast. Providentially, Tom and Margaret were planning a return visit to Northern Ireland for their daughter's wedding in 1996. Jane was to be married to Derek French, Samuel Adams brother-in-law.

At the wedding reception at the Belfast Bible College, Tom told Samuel Adams that he had come to Northern Ireland with two express purposes. The first was to give his daughter's hand in marriage to Derek; the second was to speak to Samuel Adams about the possibility of printing a million tracts to reach the boys and girls of Romania.

Following the wedding, the two men reasoned through the matter. Tom explained that he would like to have four different booklets prepared in the Romanian language: How to Get to Heaven From Romania, Good News, Find the Answer and The Way of Salvation. Tom also wanted each tract to have a tear-off slip to fill in to request a correspondence course. Samuel remembered William Carey's famous saying, "Ask great things of God. Expect great things from God." He was sure that Tom must have read these words also for this was a tall order.

After the usual prayer time on Monday morning at the EHC office Samuel shared the request with Mr. Allen. As with many other projects, Mr. Allen did not shrink from the challenge. On the contrary, he was excited by the project and could see the potential of reaching thousands of children by the printed page.

The July 1996 Newsletter of EHC carried the following report.

TWO MILLION GOSPEL TRACTS & ONE MILLION SCRIPTURE BOOKLETS were requested for Romania. The country of Romania has a population of twenty-four million people, most of whom live in the thousands of villages scattered throughout the country. This country is wide, wide open to the gospel. The people are hungry for the Word of

God. A harvest of souls is being reaped, and hundreds of new evangelical churches have been formed since the fall of Communism. However, there are still thousands of villages without a gospel witness. As soon as possible we will be supplying these millions of tracts and booklets to missionary Tom Somerville and his friends in Romania.

The first print run of these tracts was completed in two colours and immediately dispatched to Tom and his colleagues in Romania. Just about that same time Samuel Adams had opportunity to visit Hungary, Romania's western neighbour, and sensed the hunger for God's Word in Eastern Europe. He realised that the same children's tract could be used in other Eastern European countries. Upon his return to Northern Ireland he shared this burden with his colleagues and they went to work at the Every Home Crusade printing press. They published one million "God's Way of Salvation" booklets and another million children's tracts.

In November of 1996 the EHC Newsletter carried a photo of Tom and Margaret with the consignment of literature ready to be sent to Romania.

TWO MILLION GOSPEL TRACTS AND ONE MILLION SCRIPTURE BOOKLETS are being printed for Romania. Brother Somerville told us that at this time Romania is being blessed with an outpouring of the Holy Spirit. Thousands of persons have been turning to the Lord Jesus Christ as Saviour. Every week new churches are being opened. Brother Somerville and his friends have a special burden for the children of Romania, and these tracts are to be used in that ministry. Over 20,000 young people have enrolled in their Bible Correspondence Course. However, there are still thousands of villages in Romania without a gospel witness, and our friends are now preparing to make a special effort to reach the people in these villages with the gospel of our Lord Jesus Christ."

As a result of the distribution Tom and his team received many replies at the CEF office.  One little girl wrote;

Dear Mr. Somerville,

I am writing to let you know that I have received the Lord Jesus in my heart. I have many problems with my parents who do not allow me to read the Bible. Thank you that through the lessons in the Bible Correspondence Course, I know that the Lord Jesus died for me, and He has given to me eternal life. I am so happy, that I had to write this letter to tell you that I have received the Lord Jesus as my Saviour...

Viorica.

A Christian from the Republic of Moldova expressed his delight in receiving the tracts.  He wrote;

What a joy it was to receive the latest shipment of the tracts. We are especially thankful for the tracts for the young people of Moldova. As far as I know, these are the first tracts ever to be printed for the young people of Moldova, which was formerly part of the USSR, and which has a population of about five million persons. The people are very poor and have a difficult life, but their hearts are open to the gospel message. Thank you so much for your partnership in the spread of the gospel of our Lord Jesus Christ.

Within a short period of time over 34,564 young people in Romania were enrolled in Bible study courses with a further 1400 young people enrolling every month. Hundreds of young people were trusting in the Lord Jesus as Saviour through the use of tracts and the Bible courses. Repeated requests were made for another one and a half million children's tracts.

Child Evangelism Fellowship in Europe were invited to translate the material in these Mailbox Club tracts into other European languages. Eagerly they began to work, and the tract that invited children to take part in a Bible study correspondence course was translated and published in Russian, Hungarian, Italian, English-Shona, Estonian, Portuguese and Spanish and dispatched to the respective countries. Shipments of the Spanish and Portuguese tracts were also shipped to Paraguay and Brazil.

Tom reported to his prayer partners that during the following summer in Romania many Christian young people travelled by car to various outlying villages and towns where they distributed tens of thousands of these tracts. Within a short time, responses from numerous readers, young and old, came pouring into the CEF office in Sibiu. Tom organised a team of workers to individually attend to the replies and enroll the inquirers in the correspondence course.

After eight years of work in Europe Tom and Margaret were convinced that they should return to Northern Ireland. Tom had always maintained that Fermanagh was the most beautiful county in Ireland, and he was eager to return there to work with CEF. While they waited for a replacement to take over their duties in Romania, the leadership of CEF, in light of the success of their work, suggested to Tom and Margaret that they consider going to Dublin to try to implement a similar programme.

After duly considering this proposal, Tom and Margaret forwent going to Fermanagh and headed for Dublin in 1999. Initially they found it difficult to come to terms with the contrast between Dublin and Romania. The Somervilles' did not find the same spirit of evangelism in Dublin that they had experienced in Romania.

Tom and Margaret's work in Dublin was rudely interrupted when Tom suffered a heart attack in the spring of 2001. The situation was further complicated when Tom was also diagnosed with a malignant lymphoma in August of the same year. The news not only shocked the whole family, it brought great changes to all their lives.

Throughout the next two and a half years of Tom's medical treatment he never lost his love for the Saviour nor his enthusiasm and passion for the work in Romania.  The work there continued to make great advances and under the leadership of Linda Corry, the CEF team increased to forty full-time workers.   Margaret and the girls surrounded Tom with their love and care until he went to be with Christ on 2nd January 2004.

Prior to his death Tom wrote from his hospital bed,

I am a patient in Craigavon Hospital where I am receiving chemotherapy for a life threatening cancer. But I am at peace. My life is not threatened, only my body is. Jesus said, "I am the resurrection and the life, he that believeth in me though he were dead, yet shall he live, and whoever liveth and believeth in me shall never die." I believe this truth with all my heart because Jesus said it. I gladly accept God's will for my life. To live - GOOD. To die - BETTER.
Dear Friend, don't "bank" on life. It is incredibly short. Only a few reach eighty. Many die younger. Some in their twenties, thirties, forties, etc. People die at all ages. Don't "bank" on life. "Bank" on death. It's a certainty. Be ready. To experience true life on this earth you must come to Christ. You must live God's way. Jesus says, "He that has the Son has life. He that has not the Son of God has not life."
The secret to real life is in Christ. Life is that simple. I wish I had discovered it at a younger age. All the best. I hope you experience real life.

Tom Somerville lived every minute to the full.  He fought a good fight, ran a great race and kept the faith. Today he enjoys the fullness of life at the Saviour's side.  He is survived by Margaret, his five daughters and three precious grandchildren.

# Facts about
## Every Home Crusade

- Printing gospel literature in 90 Languages

- Supplying missions, churches, pastors and Christian workers in 120 countries with free supplies of evangelistic literature.

- 880 Tonnes of paper was used in the Gospel Literature factory during 2004.

- 20 Million Gospel of John booklets have been printed during the last two years.

- Each month we send 18 Tonnes of Literature in a container to India in an effort to reach the millions of souls in this vast nation.

- 30 % of our literature is sent to African countries.

- 86,000 Sets of Children's Bible Lessons have been produced in the last year.

- 25% of our literature is sent to Central and South America in the Spanish and Portuguese languages.

- This ministry is supported entirely by gifts from supporters. To operate this ministry we need to receive on average £3,000.00 per day – seven days a week throughout the year.

- Countries currently waiting for container loads of literature: - Russia, Ukraine, Nigeria, Ghana, Liberia, Kenya, Tanzania, Ethiopia, Zambia, Congo, Philippines, India, Paraguay, Brazil, Colombia, Venezuela, Honduras, Nicaragua.

*Contact details:*
**Every Home Crusade**
2 Clara Street,
Belfast,
BT5 5GB,
N. Ireland.

Telephone: **028 9045 5026**

Website: **revivalmovement.org**